KU-655-330

THE SUITCASE

BY THE SAME AUTHOR

Who Paid the Piper?
The CIA and the Cultural Cold War

Hawkwood: Diabolical Englishman

The Woman Who Shot Mussolini

THE SUITCASE

Six Attempts to Cross a Border

Frances Stonor Saunders

JONATHAN CAPE

LONDON

1 3 5 7 9 10 8 6 4 2

Jonathan Cape, an imprint of Vintage, is part of the
Penguin Random House group of companies whose addresses
can be found at global.penguinrandomhouse.com

Penguin
Random House
UK

Copyright © Frances Stonor Saunders 2021

Frances Stonor Saunders has asserted her right to be identified
as the author of this Work in accordance with the Copyright,
Designs and Patents Act 1988

First published by Jonathan Cape in 2021

penguin.co.uk/vintage

A CIP catalogue record for this book is available from
the British Library

ISBN 9781787330542

Typeset in 11/14 pt Stempel Garamond
by Integra Software Services Pvt. Ltd, Pondicherry

Printed and bound in Great Britain by Clays Ltd, Elcograf S.p.A.

The authorised representative in the EEA is Penguin Random House Ireland,
Morrison Chambers, 32 Nassau Street, Dublin D02 YH68

Penguin Random House is committed to a sustainable future for
our business, our readers and our planet. This book is made from
Forest Stewardship Council® certified paper.

Something hidden. Go and find it. Go and look behind the Ranges –
Something lost behind the Ranges. Lost and waiting for you. Go!

Rudyard Kipling, 'The Explorer'

There are the Alps …
you will have to go a long way round
if you want to avoid them.

Basil Bunting, 'On the Fly-Leaf of Pound's Cantos'

For my brothers, Alexander and Hugo

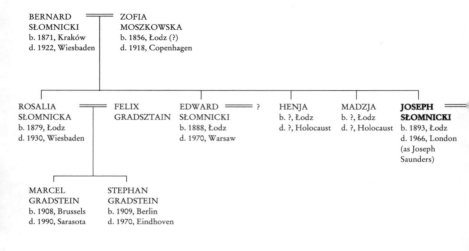

BERNARD
SŁOMNICKI
b. 1871, Kraków
d. 1922, Wiesbaden

ZOFIA
MOSZKOWSKA
b. 1856, Łodz (?)
d. 1918, Copenhagen

ROSALIA
SŁOMNICKA
b. 1879, Łodz
d. 1930, Wiesbaden

FELIX
GRADSZTAIN

EDWARD
SŁOMNICKI
b. 1888, Łodz
d. 1970, Warsaw

?

HENJA
b. ?, Łodz
d. ?, Holocaust

MADZJA
b. ?, Łodz
d. ?, Holocaust

JOSEPH
SŁOMNICKI
b. 1893, Łodz
d. 1966, London
(as Joseph
Saunders)

MARCEL
GRADSTEIN
b. 1908, Brussels
d. 1990, Sarasota

STEPHAN
GRADSTEIN
b. 1909, Berlin
d. 1970, Eindhoven

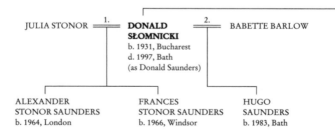

JULIA STONOR

1.

DONALD
SŁOMNICKI
b. 1931, Bucharest
d. 1997, Bath
(as Donald Saunders)

2.

BABETTE BARLOW

ALEXANDER
STONOR SAUNDERS
b. 1964, London

FRANCES
STONOR SAUNDERS
b. 1966, Windsor

HUGO
SAUNDERS
b. 1983, Bath

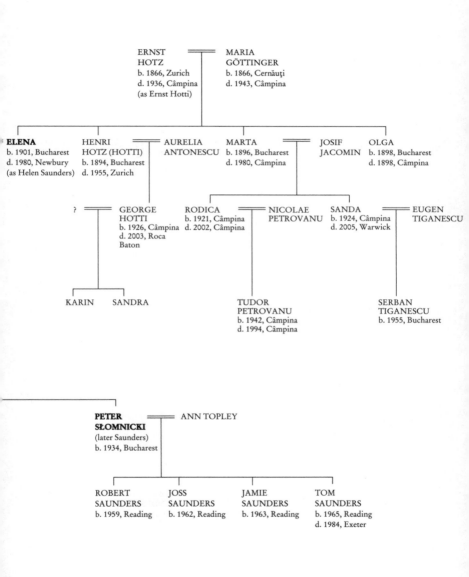

ONE

Are we to believe then, father, there are souls
Who rise from here to the sky of the upper world
And re-enter the sluggish drag of the body?
What possesses the poor souls? Why this mad desire
To get back to the light?

Seamus Heaney, *Aeneid Book VI*

THE SUITCASE ARRIVED long after its owner had left. It was handed over to me ten years ago in the car park of a London church on a miserable, gun-metal-grey morning of rain and tears. The suitcase is chalk-coloured, weather-speckled, hooped with wooden struts that have warped. It smells of damp and the stale vapours of the past. It's fastened by two rusty lockable latches but there are no keys, so it may have to be prised open. I haven't tried. It is very heavy and I loaded it into my car with difficulty. My mother, who was with me that day, was unusually quiet as I drove her home. She simply said, 'If you open that suitcase you'll never close it again.'

While enjoying certain kinds of complication (seating mourners correctly at a funeral, insulting someone with a second-class stamp, genealogy), my mother has a pronounced aversion to others (washing up, replacing a battery, packing or unpacking a suitcase), but I suspect her comment was directed at a larger possibility of difficulty than the merely practical. I didn't ask because I didn't want to talk about it. I put the suitcase in her attic and then, some months later, my uncle agreed to take it to his house, where he put it in his attic. I didn't want it in my attic. I still don't. Not yet.

The suitcase belonged to my father. He died in 1997, aged sixty-five, although he'd been finessing his final disappearing act for almost a decade, since the doctor first told him he had Alzheimer's. After the diagnosis, he had written the word on a yellow Post-it and stuck it in his diary, in case he forgot the name of the condition that makes you forget everything. The illness seemed to become more aggressive once he knew he had it. Time, distance, objects, people – every landmark on his mental map skewed several degrees out. 'This is very good, I can recommend it. You cut it up and it's sort of hard on the edges and really quite delicious. I can't remember what it's called.' 'It's a loaf of bread.'

Every morning my father walked the dog. One day he forgot the dog and took the lead for a walk. Whenever he realised something was awry, he would rush off to look for his diary with the yellow Post-it. This was his polar north, and as long as it could be located, he seemed to be in contact – just – with a reality that was slipping away. Sometimes, inevitably, he would lose the Post-it, and then he would painstakingly write out a new one. Gradually, he lost track of how the letters were organised, and the word began to fall to pieces:

A-L-Z-H-E-I-M-E-R-S
A-Z-H-I-E-M-E-R-L-S
A-H-Z-S-M-I-E-L-E-R

And then all the words fell to pieces. At some point he forgot how to speak. Occasionally a few words would come out, but they didn't make sense, there was no longer a context. Only his physical habits remained intact – the way he walked; how he organised his hair so it didn't flop on the wrong side; the way he took his handkerchief out of his pocket and tied a knot in it. He'd always done this to remind himself of something – but now, what?

When it looked really bad, his second wife brought him back from the care home, where there was care, but no home. In the last few days he took no fluid and his lips dried and peeled like old paint. The nurse moistened them with a cotton bud dipped in water. He rattled all the time, and the distance between breaths became longer. You would lean in close to his mouth and count to ten, eleven, twelve, thirteen seconds, and still no breath. Just when you thought he must be dead, it came back again, a long, drain-emptying gurgle, and you would pull back in surprise.

I went to the local Benedictine abbey to collect the old abbot who had agreed to give the Last Rites to my father, who wasn't a Catholic, but he wouldn't have minded. It was a dank, slushy evening, and I had difficulty seeing the road. I didn't know what to talk about, so I asked the abbot to tell me what the Seven Deadly Sins were. 'Gee. Gosh! Let me think.' He could only name four. I had the impression he was slightly demented himself. He stumbled a few times while reading the Last Rites and we got the giggles. He left, and my father continued rattling until the next evening and then the breathing really did stop.

We put a wild flower from the garden in his hands and folded them on his chest. His fingers were the same colour as the yellowed enamel of the stove in the kitchen, but his face started to fill out a bit, as if the blood was making one final, defiant circuit through his capillaries. For an instant the deep worry-lines on his brow vanished and he settled into a dead calm. He looked surprisingly well. 'What's it like?' I wanted to ask him. 'Do you feel better now?'

The undertakers zipped him into a mauve body-bag and took him away. A few days later, Alexander, my older brother, went to the funeral home – all these homes, this last being the least homely – to choose a coffin. He reported that Daddy had been installed in a garage, which, it had been stressed, was modified to mortuary standards. We bundled up his clothes and shoes in a couple of black bin liners and took them to the charity shop. I imagined, in those mystifying days after his death, while he was still lying in the refrigerated garage and normal time had been put on ice, that we would sort through his stuff, but this never happened.

I do have a few things that belonged to him: two silver sixpences I had found in a much earlier clear-out when he and my stepmother were moving house. The coins were in the top pocket of his National Service uniform, which went in the skip, along with a little glass duck, which he kept retrieving but finally relinquished when we insisted it wasn't worth keeping. It kept bobbing to the surface, and I began to feel guilty, so I saved it. Other things have found their way to me in the years since his death – his stamp albums, some photographs, books about mountains – and, of course, the suitcase that I haven't opened.

The suitcase is too big and unwieldy to be the one my father carried when he crossed the border out of his childhood and discovered just how sad a place the world can be. I don't know at what point in his life he acquired it. It just fetched up in an attic and became a convenient thing for putting things in, which is what a suitcase is. All I've been told is that it's crammed with paper – correspondence, documents, photographs – and that my stepmother didn't want to go through it. This, then, is my awkward inheritance: the remains of the confusions and scatterings of a life lived in dispersal.

Until recently I didn't think about the suitcase at all, but then it suddenly occurred to me that this has been a sort of effortful non-thinking; that for a long time I have been concentrating on forgetting it. Strangely, I have forgotten what it was that brought me to this realisation. I only remember the lurching sensation that accompanied it, like being heaved up by a speed bump you haven't seen because you're fiddling with the car radio.

Now, I find myself living inside the dilemma of two competing urges: wanting to know what's in the suitcase, and wanting not to know. My hope is that, if I open it, the suitcase may offer a way across a border to meet my father, who in life was unknowable to me. A gap in the wall, a hole in the wire will do. Then maybe I could restore something – what? – from the dislocation. But I hesitate at the threshold of this journey; it fills me with misgivings. 'Know your limits': how often did I hear adults say this to me in my childhood, only ever delivered as an impeachment for some or other extramural behaviour. I've never appreciated being told to know my limits but I have come to recognise, even if I don't easily accept, that borders are places of risk and we cross them at our peril. They are *sacred*, 'set apart', defined precisely by division, which is why we hold their defence to be sacrosanct. We teach ourselves the limits of our lives by beating the bounds – literally so, in the past; today, mostly symbolically, and often so habitually that we are not conscious of doing it. And here we stand, apart.

From my father's extreme economy in talking about the past, I always knew there was much he wanted to forget, and yet the suitcase tells me he had not embraced the art of letting go. If I rummage around in his world, his things, I might see more than I can take in, I might meet the private turmoil that made a relationship with him so contingent, so fragile. Or I may find treasure, a gift that will substitute for whatever it was I felt the lack of, the loss of. Perhaps this is the greater risk: of finding something over nothing, of realising that what I most wanted was always there.

I remember, with a disquieting clarity that includes the weave of the carpet under my bare feet, the moment I discovered my father's love letters to my mother. I was about ten, mooching around his post-divorce home in Wiltshire and in a furtive mood. He was gardening and I was peeved that he had not clocked how the hours drag for a bored child. Having nothing better to do, I lowered the drop-front of his Georgian desk and started to pull open the tiny drawers. Pens, pencils, elastic bands, paper clips, stamps – Thackeray's knick-knackeries, what you would expect to find in a desk. But then a bundle of letters tied with string, which I carefully untied after turning to note the position of the figure outside pushing the lawn-mower. His back was turned, a familiar sight.

'Darling Dodo', followed by flumes of love in his tiny, cramped writing, overrunning at the end of each letter and seeking out the narrow margin upwards, over the top, downwards on the other side. That there had ever been any love or tenderness between my parents was, until this point, a carefully withheld secret. It was, to me, an unimaginable hinterland to the storms of furious shouting, slamming doors, frozen silence. There was no pleasure or comfort to be taken from the revelation. I had stolen a look at the letters, and they had robbed me of the story I had made my home in, replacing it with something entirely uncanny, *unheimlich*, unhomely.

As a child, I was dimly aware of a series of shatterings that had torn people from their lives. There was Cousin Katya, who had once lived somewhere as a countess but was now confined to one room in grungy (it was in the 1970s) South Kensington. This, my mother explained, was a bedsit, which made sense, as the bed was needed for sitting on. On the back wall there was a rudimentary free-standing kitchen behind a curtain that ran on a sagging U-shaped plastic track. Down the corridor there was a bathroom shared with other bedsitters and a separate chamber for the loo, with a wall-mounted cistern from which dangled a long chain with an ancient brass handle in the shape of a pine cone, though it closely resembled a turd and I was always loath to pull it. Katya had no money, so she made beautiful ceramic plates and sold them. She spoke to my mother of various people she used to know in her other life and was very dismissive of a princess, Someone-Metternich, who had escaped (from what, I did not know) with a wheel-barrow filled with her jewels.

There were more vivid encounters with severance, whose cause I slowly came to recognise as 'the war'. Sean Crampton had lost a leg (his prosthetic replacement, which was always attached to the same brown brogue, he used to place behind a curtain at night, with only the foot showing, to deter intruders); Roger Lloyd had lost an arm (I initially thought that his huge dog, Gozo – so fierce that he had to be housed in a derelict tennis court – had torn it from its socket and eaten it); Robert Crabbe had lost several toes, which I did not think too serious until he explained they were required for balance (I understood balance in the negative context of not having enough of it, hence those shameful stabilisers fastened to my bicycle).

At some point I was given to understand that the back-drop to the war was a preceding war, the First World War – pronounced by my cut-glass maternal grandmother as the '*Fast* World War' – a very messy affair that had made Harry Clack's lungs turn green. Harry worked in the potting sheds of my mother's ancestral home and hacked up an eternal spew of mustard-gas phlegm. This got him out of going to the second war, which was a replay of the first, but bigger, though some people we knew, like Canon Pickering, had been in both.

These wars were as distant to me in early childhood as Battersea Fun Fair, which occupied a far greater part of my consciousness and whose attractions, much vaunted by my older brother Alexander, who had actually been there, I was never to experience. I had no idea that my father, limbs intact, had been clobbered by the same event that had separated Sean from his leg, Roger from his arm, and Robert from his toes. I had no idea, as he poured sherry for the vicar after church on Sunday, that my father was anything other than a 'from here' person. Donald Saunders looked the same and sounded the same as the other guests who sipped Tio Pepe (medium or dry) from Lilliputian glasses and did small-talk while Alexander and I handed around the shiny peanuts (bald, like the vicar), after first shovelling out fistfuls for ourselves.

True, Daddy's mother was different. She spoke with a heavy accent, recited proverbs in several languages we couldn't understand, and sighed for places and things that were long lost to her. She was obviously misplaced in our impeccably English life, a foreigner whose existence was shaped and organised around neuralgic points labelled *Apfelstrudel* and *Rrree-shart Schtrauss*. To humour her, we had to watch the whole of the televised Vienna Philharmonic New Year's Concert (nostalgia by calendar), which was infinitely boring, while she hummed the *gemütlich* waltzes and lifted her tear-filled eyes to the heavens somewhere above her son's low-beamed Wiltshire ceiling, saying, *Mein Gott, mein Gott*.

Despite absorbing my grandmother's foreignness as an established fact – I was vaguely conscious that she came from the Austro-Hungarian Empire, which had spa towns and 'concert palaces' and didn't exist any more – it hadn't occurred to me to extend this perception to my father, who sounded English and whose idea of dressing down at the weekend was to wear a cravat instead of a tie, even when mowing the lawn. I call in evidence the shirt collar-stiffeners and cufflinks, the classic Oxford shoes from Jermyn Street, the G. F. Trumper's shaving soap in a wooden bowl, the City office with highly polished desk and leather blotters and wood panelling and the secretary in an anteroom who patched us through on the telephone, the beautifully trimmed Rover Coupé with crackled leather seats, the subscription to *The Spectator*, the pot of Gentleman's Relish in the fridge.

What you think you know, you do not know. I was completely unaware that my father had an accent until I was at university, when a friend, after meeting him, asked me where he was from. There it was, the soft, rolling, back-of-the-throat 'R', escaping like a gentle breeze through the imperfect, defensive construction of Englishness – of course I'd heard it, all my life I'd heard it, but until that moment I had never heard it as a register of foreignness. The word 'foreign' has its roots in Latin: *fores*, 'door', and then *foris* or *foras*, 'outside'. Suddenly a door swung open and I saw him, not so much as a stranger, for he had always been that, but as a stranger situated in the flora and fauna of his foreignness.

Of course I had seen, next to the Gentleman's Relish, the box of finely dusted Turkish delight, the halva, the packets of rösti; I had been with my father to his birthplace in Romania and seen the locations of his childhood, not once but twice; together with Alexander, I had been in the ancient forests with him, had picked wild raspberries and cracked open hazelnuts with a stone. I had helped him fill the box of Christmas gifts for our cousins stuck there behind the Iron Curtain – chocolate, vitamins, medicine, Marmite, jam, tinned sardines, powdered soup, stockings. But through some trick of separation, these things had featured only in the margin of my map of my father. At least until that day when my friend asked: 'Where's your father from?' More than thirty years have passed, and still I hover in the same state of postponed understanding, like the delayed response between the turning of a ship's wheel or the pulling of a bell rope. Where was he from? Why do I need to know? Will I feel better if I do?

When I think of thinking back, I hear a record on the turntable. My father has left the room – being there was only ever a prelude to leaving – and I sit alone, a young girl, listening with mounting anxiety to the strains of a Romanian pan flute. This is the music of restless souls: urgent, melancholic skids in a minor key, an unending complaint so depressing at times that one of its greatest exponents, Rezsö Seress, best known for his song 'Gloomy Sunday', tried to kill himself by jumping out of a window (on a Sunday). To this day I cannot bear to hear this music. It is made by ghosts dragging chains – and suitcases – miserable and unloved. The dead cannot speak, but they tell us something, over and over: *Remember we are dead.* What are we supposed to do about that?

My father was always making lists. It was, I think, a kind of actuarial, over-determined attempt to forfend the unexpected, part of a larger scheme to organise the world around fixed points. There were lists of the days we were scheduled to spend with him, made months in advance and photocopied for those whom it concerned – Alexander, me, our mother, our boarding schools, so they knew who would be picking us up and taking us back. There were lists of Christmas presents: to whom, how much spent, from whom, thank-you letters written, thank-you letters pending. And there were always lists of things before a journey.

In the early stages of his dementia, when everything that was very far away seemed to come closer, he announced as we were washing up after a Sunday lunch that he was writing a memoir of his childhood. He went to his study and returned with a list, which ran to about eight bullet points covering a quarter of a sheet of ruled A4. I remember only a line about picking wild raspberries, and another about chasing a wheel as it bounded through a field of maize after falling off the car in which he was being driven by his father. I merely glanced at the page as he dangled it before me (it was awkward, my hands were still in the soapy water), encouraged him to keep writing and said he must find a safe place for his notes, it would be a pity to lose them. Stupid advice, on reflection, because he probably put the sheet of A4 in a carefully selected – and immediately forgotten – new place. Inevitably it was lost, though I suppose it's not impossible that, like the glass duck, it resurfaced. It may have found its way into the suitcase.

In the time I have not been looking in the suitcase, I have been consulting other sources – my father's younger brother, Peter, now a robust eighty-seven; family photographs; the stamp albums; public records; other people's suitcases; books; barely legible notes despatched to me by my mother, who has a macular hole and a keen memory and styles herself 'Research Department'. All this is the kind of stuff that gives us the method for organising our ignorance of the past. It's what Hilary Mantel calls:

the record of what's left on the record. It's the plan of positions taken, when we stop the dance to note them down. It's what's left in the sieve when the centuries have run through it – a few stones, scraps of writing, scraps of cloth. It's no more 'the past' than a birth certificate is a birth, or a script is a performance, or a map is a journey.

We can never fully retrieve the past from these relics – a blessing, surely, as the past in all its detail would overwhelm the present – but it doesn't stop us trying.

BEGINNINGS

Two births. The first is Greater Romania, conceived after complicated coitus at the Paris Peace Conference 1919, safely delivered as the fifth-largest country in Europe, June 1920. Doomed to success. The second birth is Donald Robin Słomnicki, in a small town near Bucharest on 3 February 1931. Father, Joseph Słomnicki, of Polish-Russian Jewish parentage, nationalised British; mother, Elena Słomnicki, née Hotz, Austrian-German-Swiss, not Jewish, nationalised British. Both are educated in war and the packing of suitcases and the sheer shiftiness of borders. Home is something that comes and goes, it is a for-now place.

And, for now, Joe and Elena are doing quite well. They have their first, long-awaited child, and a newly built villa at the edge of Câmpina, a fast-expanding town beside an oilfield forty miles north of the capital. Photographs show Elena arranging flowers in the sitting room; Joe sitting in an armchair next to the ceramic-tiled stove, half in shadow (I wonder: are these the shadows of the past or the future?); Joe outside, surveying the newly planted garden. Donald is photographed wrapped in a towel after a bath, grappling with potty training, lying on his back having an important conversation with a teddy bear. Another baby appears,

Peter, in 1934. The saplings in the garden have grown several feet. Joe fixes up a swing and a climbing pole.

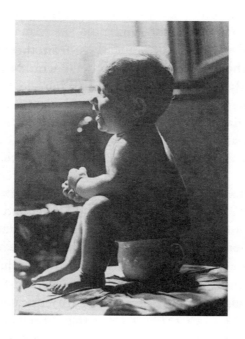

Childhood is lived not in history but in geography, in the slow, systematic mapping of place. Every child is a pioneer, surveying with great seriousness a world in which everything is new under the sun. There is a door, there is a room; there is a window where the sun pours in and the vase of flowers is broken by its rays; there is the tiled stove, cold to the touch in summer, hot in winter, which is confusing; there are stairs to be investigated, initially on all fours, and halfway down the stairs is a stair where you sit, there isn't any other stair quite like it. There is another door, another room, a bed and the space under the bed that waits to be explored, but only by the brave. Slowly, after many disorienting journeys, the mysteries are resolved, one place leads to another and the pattern of the world at hand is revealed.

The geography lesson continues outside, in the garden with its swing and climbing pole, its young trees and borders filled with tulips, and then beyond, in the broad street on the other side of the picket fence, in a pram, then on unsteady feet, and eventually on a bicycle, but only on the pavement and *do not cross the road until I get there*. The command is delivered in German by Elena or the Austrian nanny. Romanian is for tradesmen or earthy servants who, given the chance, will whisper dark secrets in your ear.

Excursions further afield are taken in the family car, a four-door Adler saloon, whose wheel will come loose one day and Donald will have to give chase as it romps through a field. Elena sits in the front and feels carsick. Joe tells her to keep her eyes on a fixed point in the distance and suck a boiled sweet. The boys loll in the back, their bare legs sticking to leather seats heated by the sun. It takes about an hour to reach a mountain valley near Sinaia, where chestnut trees, maples and hornbeam flourish. They leave the car and take a track that leads past huge oak trees with roots covered in deep moss and giant fungi, before climbing up through beech woods, then forests of pine and larch. There are streams flecked with tiny flakes of gold. They are overtaken by flocks of long-legged sheep seeking the high pastures, accompanied by shepherds wearing tall black hats and long sheepskin coats, worn shaggy-side in. Eventually they reach the bright-green meadows on top of the mountain and set out a picnic. Beyond lie the spectacular grey peaks of the Carpathians.

Joe is doing well in the oilfields and has purchased a holiday cottage in the village of Poiana. In winter he teaches Donald to ski (Peter is too small, and by the time he is big enough the mountains will be beyond reach). There are no ski-lifts, so they have to walk up through the treeline where the snow is less deep, carrying their clunky wooden skis and poles. They work on ploughing and carving, sharp christies, controlled avoidance, until Donald is ready to be unleashed, speeding down the course at the edge of the forest, arriving at the bottom in what seems a fraction of a second, breathless, eyes watering, triumphant. Later, as the sun dips behind the mountains, he sits by the stove with a mug of hot chocolate and listens to the baying of not-so-distant wolves while Joe waxes the skis for tomorrow.

In the foothills of these mountains are the oil refineries of Ploieşti, where Joe works. He is a geologist who reads the rocks after splitting them with a special pickaxe, and they tell him where the oil is. He used to work around the fringes of the big fields with his friend Robin Redgrave, but this was a boom-and-bust affair and Joe has since taken up a position with Steaua Romana, a subsidiary of British Petroleum. Robin's son, Roy, is Donald's best friend. Occasionally the two boys are allowed to accompany their fathers to Ploieşti, a short, bumpy drive from Câmpina along a rutted dirt road that follows the streams uphill until the unmistakable tang of crude oil hits the nostrils and the immense wooden derricks appear over the silver-birch trees.

Oil is always surrounded by people who want some of it, and everybody is here: French, Dutch, Italians, Austrians, Bulgarians, Turkish, British, Americans. During their lunch break the local men on site eat cold *mămăliga*, a maize-flour dish, and tell stories of their wartime adventures and how packs of wolves were seen in their village last winter. On one occasion Roy watches Texan oil drillers as they walk with a pistol in each hand, keeping a square jerrycan rolling ahead of them by firing well-aimed shots at the top corners.

The Redgraves live a few miles from Câmpina, in a large house overlooking the River Doftana. Roy, his sisters Ioana and Mary Maud, Donald and toddler Peter roam the garden and orchard, picking apples, peaches, apricots and cherries; they hide in the summerhouse and make camps in the woods – carefree, unchaperoned by anxious mothers (Elena, for some reason, is always fearing the worst) and studiously avoiding the hot-tempered nanny with a jingling bunch of keys tied to her belt, who rules the Doftana house. In winter they toboggan down the steep slopes into the valley, and on the way up for another run they watch as blocks of ice are cut out of the river and dragged into a pit dug deep into the hillside, where it is stored between layers of straw; come the summer, they gaze at the painfully slow turning of the handle in the wooden ice-cream bucket as it crushes the ice in a cylinder packed with fresh fruit and cream.

Back in the house, the children drift into a large drawing room where Roy's mother Micheline, a concert pianist, sits at a grand piano on a raised dais. On the wide steps leading up to it is a huge bearskin rug, complete with taxidermied head. After this, the disenchantment of day's end: Donald and Peter are taken back to Câmpina, supper is eaten, baths taken and they are settled into their shared bedroom. A story is read, the lights are turned out and the boys fall asleep to the muffled sounds of that separate, mysterious time zone that is the adult world.

Roy's father, Robin Redgrave, was Joe's closest friend. He was also Donald's godfather. Much later, Roy was godfather to my brother, Alexander. Bear with me. Roy's wife, Valerie, was godmother to my younger brother, Hugo, Daddy's son by his second marriage (biologically, but only in that sense, he is my half-brother). Valerie and Roy's eldest son, also named Alexander, was Daddy's godson. Two families roped together in friendship and event and, without much obvious religious devotion, God.

Alexander Redgrave, who is now in his early sixties, lives quite close to me in London, but I haven't seen much of him since his parents' joint memorial service in 2011. It was after the service that I was given the suitcase, brought to me by Hugo from his mother's attic and lugged from his car to mine. It was raining, I was crying and, in the blur, the lamp posts in the church car park appeared to be melting.

A few weeks ago I had supper with Alexander in his flat. We sat on low, plaited leather chairs that were somehow rescued from the house in Doftana and went through some of Roy's stuff – letters, photographs, the Doftana visitors' book, dated on the first page '1926–1940'. The signatures of Elena and Joe Słomnicki appear on almost every page, and there are other names I recognise.

I've also been to see my uncle Peter at his home in Oxfordshire. Together we looked at some family photograph albums that he had retrieved from the attic. I don't recall ever seeing these albums before, but most of the photographs (except for those that have fallen off their hinges, floating orphans) have been annotated in my father's hand. Peter and I gazed with a magnifying glass at the foxed prints, while his wife Ann, rising to the theme of historical retrieval, spoke of a cache of her own family's letters in the attic (she pointed upwards) that date back to the English Civil War.

Suddenly I felt overwhelmed. Peter and Ann and Poppy the dog and the steaming teapot all slipped out of focus. It was as if these dead people in the photographs were looking at me, and not the other way round. When Peter started gathering up the albums and putting them into a plastic bag, I told him I wouldn't take all the albums, just one for now – *that one* (randomly) – and I left with the plastic bag and drove back to London. The album was immediately shoved under the sofa. If I can't see it, maybe it can't see me: just like the suitcase. I do not want to live with ghosts. That night I dreamed I was on a London Underground platform, searching for the Exit sign. I followed the stream of passengers, all of whom bypassed a stationary man in a crumpled raincoat. Then everybody was gone except for this man, who was staring at the ground. It was my father. I went up to him. 'Daddy. *Daddy?*' He didn't lift his eyes, he didn't see me. 'I'm hungry,' he whispered.

There it is again: the dislocation, the dread feeling that something is in the wrong place. It's not the obvious – Donald Saunders, dead for decades, riding the Piccadilly Line – though that seems real enough. It's that, in my dreams, my father returns and I always recognise him but he never recognises me. He is not the stranger; I am.

At some point in my father's dying days I approached him at his bedside and said, 'Daddy.' Correction. What I actually said was, 'Daddy?' To my astonishment, he opened his eyes and answered with a question of his own: 'Yes?' It was the last word I heard him speak. I was hoping for a suitable ending, a deathbed scene like in the movies where the dying and the left-behind are jointly gifted a glimpse of the secret pattern that explains why we have to live in order to die – a flare of exaltation, the light that sings eternal, that sort of thing. I sat next to Daddy's bed, there was nobody else in the room and I knew there would be no other opportunity to speak privately with him (dying is surrounded by busyness), but I couldn't find the words, so I said nothing.

Two or three days after he died, I was in the basement kitchen doing nothing in particular. It was a strange time, or non-time, and I don't remember much about it except this: everybody else in the house had gone to bed, it was silent but for the humming of the fridge, and then I heard my father walking slowly but purposefully along the flag-stones of the passage leading to the kitchen door, which was shut. I was immediately aware of his intention: he wanted to talk to me. He came closer and closer, and at the point at which I knew him to be on the other side of the door, I shouted at him, 'No! Please don't. I can't. Please go away.' And he did.

Except he didn't.

The dream of my father in the Underground-underworld has immobilised me. I have been deadlocked for months, unable to do anything. Why is he haunting me? Why must I be at his beck and call? I was wrong about the dead – they do speak. They prowl the perimeters of our lives and, gaining the weak spot, they come to us in our dreams and in our memories and tell us to feed them and carry out tasks like opening their suitcases. They make Pandoras of us all, and what good can come of that?

Either I open the suitcase or I don't. It's binary; I can't half-do it, any more than Pandora could half-open the box. In any case it wasn't a box, it was a jar. Hesiod, writing in the seventh century BC, tells us that Zeus stuffed a jar (*pithos*) full of every suffering known to mortals and sent it to the house of Epimetheus, brother of Prometheus who had stolen fire from the gods. Pandora, finding herself in the house of Epimetheus, and incurably nosy as all women are, took the stopper out of the jar and let fly the spirits of strife.

A *pithos* was a large storage jar, typically partly buried in the ground, whose function was to preserve things useful to the living, such as olive oil, wine, grain. Secondarily, the *pithos* could be recycled as something useful to the dead: a really big one could be repurposed as a stone coffin, and a not-so-big one could comfortably accommodate the bones or ashes of a dead person. And from that we get to *pyxis* (possibly a sixteenth-century mistranslation of *pithos*), which means 'sepulchre' or 'casket', hence Pandora's box.

The Greeks may have perfected the art of dying, but they were no better at being dead than anybody else. Every year, during a two-day drinking festival, the souls of the dead demanded to be released from their *pithoi*. The living politely complied by opening the jars on the first day, but on the second day they anointed their doors with pitch and chewed blackthorn to keep the unruly spirits at bay. The *pithoi* were then sealed again and the spirits were, literally, stopped.

That's it. Two days. I will open the suitcase and let its contents speak, but I will protect myself by eating bitter things and then I will close it again, and that will be that.

I'll then be able to get on with my own life rather than the outlived life of somebody else. I pull the album out from under the sofa and start looking at the photographs again, pretending I'm not really that interested – *What do I care?* – and unexpectedly, timidly, the past and I seem to be agreeing friendlier terms.

Remember: everything remembered is just a story; all truth is told, or so we are told. But what about the untold truth, what about all the things my father never told us or his parents never told him – things that might have helped us to live more comfortably in the world? Who wants to be left with the silence that speaks volumes?

TWO

I speak of my early childhood, that is to say, of a vast region out of which all men emerge. Whence do I come? I come from my childhood. I come from childhood as from a homeland.

Antoine de Saint-Exupéry, *Flight to Arras*

I AM STILL studiously avoiding my father's suitcase, which, in the ten years since I was given it, has sat unopened in my uncle Peter's attic. Who knows how long it sat in other attics before that – my father died more than twenty years ago, and he had moved home many times in the previous decades. The suitcase has none of the diaspora chic of Nabokov's pigskin valise, 'an elegant, elegantly scuffed piece of luggage' once owned by his mother, who had acquired it for her wedding trip to Florence. She carried it with her when she fled Russia in 1917, arriving in London with its contents (including a handful of jewels) intact. Thirty years after her death Nabokov was still travelling with it, 'from Prague to Paris, from St Nazaire to New York and through the mirrors of more than two hundred motel rooms and rented houses, in forty-six states'. For Nabokov, it was fitting – 'logical and emblematic' – that the 'hardiest survivor' of his Russian heritage proved to be a travelling bag. I can't summon the same muscular response to my father's suitcase. I can't lift it because it's too heavy, in every sense, and I can't find any reassurance in its existence. It just makes me sad.

There are two reasons, of which I am conscious, that I have not yet opened it. The first is that, as my father appeared to know next to nothing about his family, immediate or distant, I'm assuming he never had the kind of information that might have supplied him with this knowledge. The second reason flows from the first: if the stuff in Daddy's suitcase isn't about them, it's probably about us – him, his children – and that, for me at least, threatens a reckoning.

The problem with the first reason is that it assumes too much. Maybe Daddy did come into possession of family documents, but lacked the necessary context or opportunity to shape them into an explanation of where he came from. When I asked Peter recently if he had ever spoken to his parents about the past, he answered, 'No, never.' Why not? 'Well, one of the sad consequences of what happened is that we were so rarely together again as a family. We were all trying to get on with our lives and, by necessity, we were apart. Now, of course, I have so many questions I wish I'd asked.' If there are papers answering some of these unasked questions, perhaps Daddy was simply not up to doing anything with them, leaving them in the suitcase for others to find.

The problem with the second reason – it's about us – is that, if I'm right, I might have to realign all my feelings about, and for, my father. I might have to continue what was suspended that day when I found his love letters to my mother (to my young mind, a totally implausible prelude to their hostility and estrangement), and move out of the safe place I've made in my version of the story. Auden's 'lucrative patterns of frustration' come to mind: discomfort as its own reward. It's like the battered old armchair in my brother Hugo's flat, the same chair in which my grandparents and then my father and then we, his children, have sat; it's more than a hundred years old, its springs have collapsed so that our buttocks are touching the floor, but we do not want to be rid of it because it is familiar.

What if I discover that my father loved me more than I understood, or wanted to understand? That my difficulties in understanding him, and therefore loving him (how can you love someone you don't know?), were not his fault? If so, I might have to take responsibility for something – I'm not sure what, but I fear it. For the moment I think I'll leave the suitcase where it is and concentrate on what I've found elsewhere.

There's more family history lying around than I expected. I started at the zero degree of evidence, or so I thought, but I now have several boxes of material, too much to shove under the sofa and pretend it's not there. Peter has rootled out several folders and more photograph albums from his study, while from my mother comes a steady drip-drip of information mysteriously emerging from what she calls her filing system, most of which is in unstable piles on the floor or under the kitchen table, waiting, sometimes for decades (such is the system), to be transferred to box files so weighty that the shelves they sit on have sagged and seem to wince at the burden of subjects ranging from EXHUMATION to NAZIS to VATICAN. But that's another story.

Among some papers Peter gave me a while ago is a family tree, roughly sketched in the late 1970s by one of his sons, Joss, on blue Basildon Bond notepaper. On the reverse, Joss's scribbles make it clear that he was trying to trace any living relatives and get them to answer the question 'Who Am I?' Granny Helen (Elena), having already entered the fog belt of Alzheimer's, was not up to the task. Next to her name Joss has noted: 'Granny doesn't feel like writing.'

Who Am I?
Who are you to ask?

I was always secretly furious with my father for not telling me his story (I still am, except it's no longer a secret). I knew there *was* a story because a detail would sometimes leak out, but on the rare occasions he did signal something relevant, he immediately shrank from my questions, as if I were a border guard demanding that he empty out his pockets. If telling is an act of giving over one's possessions, then yes, I was asking for something. But he wouldn't tell, or couldn't tell, so I learned not to ask any more. Perhaps he mistook this for indifference and, by way of punishing him, that's what it became. Is this why I'm writing about it all, to say sorry? Or maybe – and it's not quite the same thing – this is my attempt to make an apology, an account that will set the record straight, even though I know this is an impossible task because so much of the record is lost.

I read somewhere recently that, in genealogy, you count about twenty-five years per generation. If you go back to the early 1800s now, that's nine generations. If you follow both male and female lines backwards, you will end up with a couple of hundred individuals; but if you trace not only the direct lines, but also all siblings and their offspring, then you could easily end up with 10,000 entries on your family tree. All these someones begetting someones until we get to you and me. Sybille Bedford found the whole thing irksome: 'Did one *have* to have a parent?', which is not so much a question as a complaint. For better or worse – and there's plenty of that – we have to come from someone.

When I knew her, Granny Helen always gave the impression she came from the Austro-Hungarian Empire. Vienna was her idealised centre of civilisation, a place she visited often in her memories, so I've always assumed she grew up there. But Joss's family tree gives her birthplace as Bucharest, 18 November 1901. Her mother, Maria Göttinger, was a German-Austrian born in Cernăuţi, which is a complicated place to account for as it kept migrating between the Kingdom of Romania, the Austro-Hungarian Empire, Ukraine and Russia. You say Cernăuţi, I say Czernowitz, you say Chernivtsi, I say Czernopol. In this chafing point between East and West, they would overpaint the city's official buildings when one power succeeded another, but eventually they couldn't keep up, or they ran out of paint, so all the competing colours sat next to each other. In its Hapsburg heyday it was dubbed Little Vienna, thus confessing its nervousness at being far from the centre of things.

However, Maria Göttinger seems to have lived most of her youth in the real Vienna, until she married Ernst Hotz in 1893. He was Swiss-German, born and raised in Zurich. As a young man trained in engineering, he had moved into the oil business in Romania, his successes soon lubricated by the titles of *Cavaler* ('Sir'), and *Comandor* of the Order of the Crown. Each honour was for services to commerce, and came with an impressively large medal and a blue silk sash with instructions on how to wear it, all of which is long lost (perhaps Ernst wore the regalia in his coffin). The couple built an impeccably bourgeois villa in Câmpina and had four children, one of whom died in infancy. Elena, later Granny Helen, was the youngest.

Ernst naturalised himself and his family in 1909 (up to that point they had all been Swiss passport-holders), and a year later he changed the family name to Hotti, because

Hotz translates as 'burglar' in Romanian (whereas in German it is linked to the verb *hotzen*, 'to run fast', which is something a thief might be expected to excel in, so perhaps there is a connection). I can't fathom why my great-grandfather took so long to relieve the family of his accidentally pejorative surname, or why he bothered with naturalisation to achieve this. Naturalisation is a strange legal device that starts and ends in a contradiction: the 'natural' law of citizenship specifies a right determined by blood (*jus sanguinis*) or birth (*jus soli*, 'right of the soil', as in, sprung from the earth like a potato), so any law that overrides that – one might argue, though no one does – is itself unnatural. Ernst and Marie met neither of these qualifications and seem to have flourished in Romania without them. Their children, at least, qualified on the birth clause, but it was also true that, by blood, they were 'naturally' Austrian, 'naturally' German and 'naturally' Swiss, which sort of makes a mockery of the whole concept.

In any case, the change of name was one of the few concessions made by *Cavaler-Comandor* Hotti to naturalisation. He and his family were now Romanian on paper, but hardly inclined to *become* Romanian. They spoke and wrote in German and French, brought up their children in the traditions and family-silver refinement of Mitteleuropean culture, and surrounded themselves with Hungarian cooks and starched Austrian *Schwestern* as a bulwark against actual Romanians who were seen, in the main, as illiterate and piteously underdeveloped. So, I suppose it's true: Elena did grow up in the Austro-Hungarian Empire after all.

In 1925 she changed her nationality for the third time when she married my grandfather, Joe Słomnicki, who, on paper at least, was British. From Joe's naturalisation file at the National Archives in London, we learn that he was born in Łódź on 4 December 1893. His father, Bernard

Słomnicki, a businessman trading in oil products, and his mother, Zofia Moszkowska, were both Polish subjects, or so writes Joe on his application, but technically they weren't, because Poland didn't feature on the map in their time as anything other than a submissive fraction of the Russian empire known as Congress Poland.

As far as I can discover, everyone with the name Słomnicki came originally from a small town of the same name, fifteen miles north-east of Kraków. The Słomnickis took their name from the Hebrew for Solomon, Shlomo, 'man of peace' – the same biblical root that gives us *shalom*. They were shtetl Jews, typically shoemakers, butchers, glaziers and ironmongers. A few were farmers. Though not beyond the Pale, many were destitute, a common enough condition among Polish Jewry, but Bernard, Joe's father, seems to have belonged to the minority of merchants, bankers and factory owners who, in the mid-nineteenth century, sought their fortunes in the industrial powerhouses of Warsaw, Vilna, Kraków and Łódź.

It was in Łódź that Bernard met Zofia Moszkowska, whose family can be traced to a sixteenth-century *tsadik*, or 'righteous one', though I don't know what his name was or where he was doing his righteousness. In Zofia's time, dangling from who-knows-what genealogical offshoots, the Moszkowskis had produced a world chess champion, a physician who did important work in Indonesia on beriberi disease, a playwright and two composers: Arnold Schoenberg and the piano virtuoso Artur Rubinstein, who once played piano to Einstein's violin, though the latter had to be reprimanded for coming in four beats late.

There was also Moritz Moszkowski, a famous composer who was much admired by Franz Liszt; and Moritz's brother, Alexander, a well-known writer and philosopher who did much to bring Einstein's Theory of Relativity to a wider audience. There is good reason to believe that these were Zofia's nephews, in fact I'm pretty sure they were. Jews who remained in the Jewish faith inevitably intermarried, and Polish Jewry did this to the point that it's almost impossible to unpick the connecting threads. Zofia's mother was a Słomnicka, which means that Zofia's husband, Bernard Słomnicki, was her cousin – but to get us there one might as well be supplying directions on how to drive from Wrexham to Ulaanbaatar. It's complicated.

I haven't been able to discover when or why Bernard and Zofia hauled out of Łódź, although, as a very rich city that sat on a very poor city, it was prone to waves of industrial unrest and, as night follows day, pogroms. This might also explain why they had their two sons baptised, a form of camouflage not uncommon at the time (though rarely extended to girls). Certainly, by 1910, Bernard and Zofia were living comfortably in Wiesbaden with their five children, until the outbreak of war saw them expelled from Germany as 'Russian enemy aliens', at which point they fled to Amsterdam. The family then separated, possibly to shorten the odds of survival. Joe's sisters Henja and Rosalia, with Rosalia's two young sons, stayed in Holland; Zofia took the eldest son, Edward, to Copenhagen (why exchange neutral Holland for neutral Denmark?), while Bernard managed to take Joe and another sister, Madzja, to London, where they were all registered under the Aliens Restriction Order. Joe, now twenty-one, enrolled to study geology as a 'refugee student' at the Royal School of Mines (later, part of Imperial College London), his fees being paid by his father, who appears to have shored up some funds in England.

Edward arrived in London soon afterwards, leaving his mother alone in Copenhagen. None of them would see her again. In late 1916 both brothers were called up, Edward to the Army Service Corps and Joe to the Royal Engineers as a sapper. Like all recruits, they were required to hold a Bible and take the oath of allegiance to His Majesty King George V, his heirs and successors, but as 'foreign aliens' both were denied an officer's commission. According to Joe's army record, he was demobilised three years later with 'good character', and no medals to suggest that his intention was anything other than to stay alive.

One might well ask for whom, or what, the perpetual foreign alien Joseph Słomnicki would have felt it necessary to sacrifice his life: Poland (or Congress Poland)? Russia? England, in whose green and pleasant land, it was mooted, the new Jerusalem would rise? Not for him the ancestral sword, the chariots of fire, 'The summons to complete the task of our forefathers. To die in ditches for them.' Much more likely, the aim for this young man, my future grandfather, was simply to keep on living, away from Łódź, where the 2,000-year-old hatred was sounded by the whistles of the pogrom; away from Germany and the wheeling of armies; away from the mud and blood of the trenches and all the other spectacles invented to make us miserable.

I sent Joe's naturalisation file to my uncle Peter, who has written to say that I now know more about his father's early years than he, Peter, ever did. Come to think of it, I know more than Joe himself knew, as he was never privy to the complete dossier on his application. The last line in the folder reads: 'The [Special Branch] report on the applicant and his reference is rather unfavourable, but not sufficiently as to justify a refusal.' There had been a fine for not shading a lamp during the blackout, a contested debt with a landlady in Maida Vale, a 'defective' statement of residence – small infringements, but enough, on a bad day, to stop a young Polish Jew from passing through the eye of the Home Office needle. The paperwork was stamped on 15 January 1921. Joe Słomnicki had scraped a British passport, and it would save his life.

As for what Joe intended to do with his British passport, there is a clue in his naturalisation file. There, it is noted, Joe's desired 'profession as oil-mining engineer will almost necessarily cause him to live abroad, and when questioned on this point, he astutely replied that there were oil-fields and industries within the British Dominions'. Next to this there is a scribble in another hand: 'His profession will take him abroad no doubt but there is no reason to suppose that he will not regard this country as his home.'

I don't think that last bit is right. Joe had studied in London, he'd made many friends (his firstborn son, Donald, would be named after one of them) and for three years he'd fought in the uniform of the British Army, but he had no property or assets or family in England. I don't believe he thought of it – then or later – as home, so much as a homeland in reserve. A British passport was an amulet, a premium insurance. It also offered many freedoms, and in 1922, a year after he was naturalised, Joe took himself to Romania, where Western capital was pouring into the country's oil industry. There he met Robin Redgrave, and together they roamed the oil-rich Prahova valley with their pickaxes, looking for the telltale seams that would lead them to their fortunes.

Robin had arrived a year earlier, aged twenty-two, without a single technical qualification or any experience in oil exploration. The son of a British actress and actor, who struggled with their marriage (his father went on to have several more marriages, one of which produced the actor Sir Michael Redgrave), Robin was independent, handsome and adventurous. He set himself up in a wooden house next to an oilfield close to Doftana and offered his services to the drilling companies. One day he discovered a 'swimming pool', a flooded salt mine where the water was so buoyant it was impossible to sink. There, he met Micheline Capsa, who had walked the short distance from her parents' house to meet her friends at the pool. Within three weeks they were married.

Joe, who knew a thing or two about losing everything (his father's investments in oil had ended in bankruptcy), soon exchanged the insecurity of freelancing for a permanent job in Steaua Romana, a subsidiary of British Petroleum, whose director was *Comandor* Ernst Hotti. Ernst's daughter, Elena, was Micheline's friend. There are photographs of them both swimming in the salt mine, and it's possible that Joe first met her there. Less impulsive than Robin and Micheline, and doubtless carefully observed by the imposing *Comandor* and his wife, Joe and Elena courted for a few years, marrying in 1925. Soon afterwards the couple were comfortably installed in their newly built house in Câmpina.

The country they lived in was called Greater Romania, which had been a much smaller country until its borders were redrawn at the Versailles Peace Conference in 1919. Romania being a joke in diplomatic circles – 'So young, and already a Romanian!' was a favourite quip – it was something of a surprise when the country doubled its size. This success owed much to Queen Marie, who had turned up in Paris, uninvited, to woo the victors at their peace conference. Her husband, Ferdinand, may have been the king, but it was said there was only one man in Romania, and that was the queen. '*Ah, si j'étais roi,*' was her constant complaint. For a while, she was.

Marie had thrown everything she had – haute couture and chutzpah, disabling charm, well-rehearsed argument – at the task of promoting Romania's claims. 'Romania needs a face,' she told a reporter in Paris, 'and I have come to show mine.' Faced with her sophistication, quick intelligence and resolve, the frockcoats of Versailles revisited their prejudices towards her country as a Balkan outlier, mockably unreliable and backward. She helped to turn the geography around, bringing Romania away from the wild periphery to the civilised centre. At the outcome of the peace conference, the country that had previously been squashed between the Ottoman, Austro-Hungarian and Russian Empires emerged as the fifth-largest nation in Europe – a territorial gain proportionally greater than that of any other power.

The new map of Romania was beautiful and, it transpired, designed to be so. Emmanuel de Martonne, the cartographer who dealt with Romania at Versailles, was very satisfied with the aesthetic improvement, boasting that the country that previously looked 'like a set-square' was now 'round and perfect'. To achieve this perfect circle, four provinces were acquired from other countries – a total land gain of 50 per cent – along with their populations: the Austrians of Bukovina, the Russians of Bessarabia, the Bulgarians of Southern Dobruja, and the Hungarians of Transylvania and other areas (there was now more of Hungary in Romania than there was in Hungary).

It's one thing to concoct a border on a green baize table in a conference room. A young British delegate to Versailles, Harold Nicolson, described the breaking up of Hungary as a kind of parlour game:

There (in that heavy tapestried room, under the simper of Marie de Medicis [sic]*, with the windows open upon the garden and the sound of water sprinkling from a fountain and from a lawn-hose) – the fate of the Austro-Hungarian Empire is finally settled. Hungary* *is partitioned ... while the water sprinkles on the lilac outside ... They begin with Transylvania, and after some insults flung like tennis balls ... Hungary loses her South. Then Czecho-Slovakia, and while the flies drone in and out of the open windows Hungary loses her North and East. Then the frontier with Austria, which is maintained intact. Then the Jugo-Slav frontier, where the Committee's report is adopted without change. Then tea and macaroons.*

It's not clear whether Nicolson was shocked or amused by the process – do we hear him yawn? – though it was certainly more complex than his vignette suggests. It was much easier to draw lines on a map than it was to translate these lines onto the ground, about which history has surprisingly little to say, perhaps having exhausted itself with the preliminaries. This task fell to a boundary commission of seven members, five nominated by the Allies, one by Hungary, one (in this case) by Romania. They worked with the 1:1,000,000 peace-treaty maps, doing their best to relate them to other smaller-scale maps, some of which had been drawn, it was said, with more courage than measurement. In certain instances, hills, streams and other topographical features were described by names that, in the vernacular, meant 'I Don't Know' – a last vestige, in modern Europe, of maps created and passed on orally.

Caveat emptor: there were also wilful inaccuracies, too many to document. As the chief expert of the American delegation to Versailles later noted:

It would take a huge monograph to contain an analysis of all the types of map forgeries that the war and the peace conference called forth ... A perverted map was

*a life belt to many a foundering argument. It was in
the Balkans that the use of this process reached its most
brilliant climax.*

The difficulties of carrying out readjustments to the
geography of the world were further complicated by the
presence on the ground of human beings, many of whom
were not in alignment with the changes. Local populations
were encouraged to make their views known to the commissioners in show-of-hands meetings in town halls, churches
or even on the roadside, but there was no way of recon-
ciling the needs of everyone. There were protests, inevitably
– a house straddling the new frontier, front door in
Hungary, back door in Romania; a homestead cut off from
its fields; a town deprived of its railway station, factory or
pumping plant; a church or synagogue separated from its
congregation. Disgruntled locals might shout insults as a
border post was driven in (the commissioners' reports
mention, but do not dwell upon, 'grievances', 'minor inci-
dents', 'reprisals'), but the theodolite was king.

With all Romania's new frontiers settled on the ground,
the perfect circle of Emmanuel Martonne's imagination had
been realised. Eight and a half million people stepped out
of their houses and found themselves in a different country.
Sometimes we cross the border, sometimes the border
crosses us.

Elena had not been able to attend the celebrations marking
this success. While her childhood friend, Micheline, was
giving a piano recital at Queen Marie's country palace of
Cotroceni, in a room full of gilded furniture, great bronze
chandeliers and towering flower arrangements ('vulgar', said
one British visitor), Elena was languishing with a collapsed
lung in a Swiss sanatorium. I imagine the sanatorium (on

a magic mountain, surely?), the weekly X-rays (doleful shades), the long intervals of restive, unmagical thinking. Flashbacks, no doubt, to the terrifying events of November 1916 when she, just fifteen, had fled the German Army as it converged on Bucharest and the surrounding countryside.

The Romanian lines in the Carpathians had been broken by a crack mountain battalion led by a young lieutenant, Erwin Rommel, who punched an opening through which the Central Powers poured into the lowlands and swept eastwards. By the time Queen Marie's getaway train was pulling out of Bucharest for Iaşi, just west of the Russian border, the central station was thronging with 30,000 refugees desperately trying to take the same route; those who could took cars, joining the endless, chaotic jams that were already being strafed by German Stukas; thousands more, including Micheline, the nineteen-year-old student of music, began to trudge north in the bitter cold towards the distant mountains.

Trains play a large part in this story, and it would be comforting to think that Elena had found a place on Queen Marie's train, which was packed with members of the royal family, servants, courtiers and their families, including Princess Ştirbei with her four daughters. But according to a confused story that has filtered through the rusting sieve of family memory, Elena and her older sister Marta, who was twenty, were left to make good their own escape. The roads around Câmpina were clogged with refugees, and the sisters huddled over each other in a horse-drawn cart, close enough to the German advance to see it and, behind them, black clouds of asphyxiating gas pouring out of the largest petroleum tank in Europe. The sisters clutched each other and the small treasures they were carrying, as barter for their lives. Whatever else might have been cashed in, Elena managed to hold on to

41

a twenty-two-carat chain-link gold bracelet, which I was later to inherit.

I've no idea why Elena's parents do not figure in this story. No sign either of her brother, Henri. Did they remain in Câmpina to protect their home – if you leave during a war, the enemy will smash everything and shit in your saucepans – or did they manage to follow the girls to the Russian border once the full disaster had unfolded? Either way, Elena's sinister souvenir of her first flight from home was the tuberculosis that collapsed her lung. The family all survived the war, but with who knows what kind of hidden wounds. I doubt they ever spoke about it.

In late 1920, after a year in the sanatorium, Elena returned to the newly enlarged Romania, where there was room – lots of it, just look at the map – for optimism. She met Joe, they got married and launched themselves onto the cocktail circuit and fancy-dress parties of the largely expatriate community that was producing and riding the oil boom of Greater Romania. Principal stage for these gatherings was a country estate perched on a plateau overlooking the River Doftana, just outside Câmpina. This was the parental home of Elena's dear friend, Micheline, now married to Robin Redgrave. Micheline was beautiful, talented and fun. She was also well connected, part of the small elite – royal courtiers, bankers, diplomats, industrialists – who were fuelling Romania's drive towards the greatness conferred by the ageing gentlemen of Versailles.

Greater Romania may have looked good on paper, but in reality it was an untidy, raw ethnic omelette. The task of binding all these foreigners into a cohesive nation-state fell to the Hohenzollern monarchy, a recent German import and therefore also foreign. The Hohenzollerns couldn't even speak Romanian properly, but were forgiven because they brought prestige to the country. 'I grew up ... in the belief that our glory, like that of the sun, was an unquestioned reality,' said Queen Marie, and it was she, more than Ferdinand, her ineffectual husband, who embodied the post-war aspirations of Romania, previously a *lieu de passage*, but now comfortably installed on the map as something great. Often seen dressed up in local costume ('sacrificing elegance for patriotism,' in her words), Marie positioned herself convincingly as the mother of her people, the vast majority of whom were dirt-poor but seemed not to resent her collection of palaces and castles. She also collected kings for sons-in-law, grafting two of her three daughters – the Hohenzollern rootstock – onto the crowns of Yugoslavia and Greece (narrowly losing out on Bulgaria for the third).

Her eldest son, Carol, was a different matter. The best his father could say of him was that he was 'like Emmenthaler cheese – excellent but for the holes'. Carol had disgraced himself during the war by deserting his army post to contract a left-handed marriage to Zizi Lambrino, with whom he had a son. He was reluctantly extracted from this union by his parents and the courts, which found it illegal, and was set up with Princess Helen of Greece and Denmark. They married and she tolerated him until a son was born seven months later (prompting a variety of rumours), at which point Carol swiftly commenced a long and scandalous affair with the hip-swinging redhead Magda Lupescu, a divorcee with expensive tastes who was whispered to be of Jewish descent.

In refusing to renounce Lupescu, Carol forfeited his right to succession, and the adulterous couple left Romania in 1925 for exile in Paris. As a result, when King Ferdinand died two years later, it was Michael, Carol's five-year-old son by Princess Helen, who was crowned under a regency. The boy-king featured on postage stamps for three years and was then unseated in a quiet coup by his father, who flew into Bucharest under cover of night (Lupescu followed later). Carol had chosen his moment carefully: his mother was out of the country – in Oberammergau, of all places, attending the Passion Play. On 8 June 1930 Carol was proclaimed king, a development rapturously received by the Romanian populace.

Elena Słomnicki, barely one month pregnant with her first child and therefore unaware of the fact (such are the dispensations of history, that we get to know before she does), cannot have welcomed the coup. As a teenager she had been a frequent visitor to the palace of Buftea, the principal seat of Marie's lover, Prince Barbu Ştirbei. On one occasion Elena had come down with a fever and was confined to bed (I later learned from her niece that she was 'sickly and spoilt, or vice versa') and, to alleviate the boredom, Ştirbei's wife, Nadèje, appeared in her room one morning with a beautifully ornamented box, from which she extracted a series of dazzling jewels and spread them over Elena's counterpane. She then left Elena to admire this little selection of the crown jewels of Queen Marie, who was presumably attending to other affairs.

Having been warmed, however modestly, by the sun of Marie's court, Elena could hardly wish for the shadow that was now cast over it, as Carol, jealous and resentful, moved to eclipse the influence of his mother and her lover. Marie, fearsome wartime consort of King Ferdinand, 'mother-in-law of the Balkans', was starved of finances and left to arrange flowers in her several palaces, while the indispensable Prince Ştirbei was forced into exile. Greater Romania was now the stage for a vain and feckless man who was fixated with uniforms. Carol personally redesigned them every year, paying particular attention to headgear – visor hats, fore-and-afts, pompom kepis, berets, bearskins, plumed helmets. The kitsch of Greater Romania under his rule qualifies for what Susan Sontag called 'failed seriousness': one visiting journalist who was granted an interview with the king was astonished to encounter an aide-de-camp in full military rig, 'a Hollywood ensemble of bright blue and red, golden braid and tassels, and shining, clanking sword'. A joke making the rounds implied that corsets and lipstick were also part of the officers' uniform. This silliness Carol ran as a business, the profits added to the vast fortune he was later alleged to have laundered out of the country.

Taking on the task of his mother, though without her blessing, to realise the glorious destiny of the Hohenzollerns, Carol embarked on a major enlargement of the royal palace in Bucharest, a gloomy two-storey building that was not admired by anyone. Greater Romania demanded a fitting ceremonial centrepiece, and to that end he set about demolishing the entire area to create a square big enough to parade its achievements. As he fussed over plans for his neoclassical palace, oblivious to the fact that new nations tend to express themselves through a pastiche of antiquity, others foraged the millennia to find a past that might legitimise the present.

Confirmation of Romanian-ness, it was alleged, lay in Trajan's Imperial Roman province of Dacia, whose inhabitants had outlived the Roman occupation and maintained unbroken settlement in Transylvania. There was some confusion in this thesis: on the one hand, it was said that Romania's biological patrimony came directly from the local tribes of 2,000 years ago who had avoided contamination by the Romans; on the other hand, or hands, it was said that true Romanians were descended from the bastards begot from Dacian women who had succumbed to the dashing Roman conquerors, and/or Rome had simply forgotten to bring her soldiers home in AD 274 when

Emperor Aurelian withdrew from Dacia, and/or Rome didn't want to repatriate the garrison of this hardship post in the northern wall of the empire because it had gone rogue. Regardless, it was the Latinity of these Transylvanian ancestors that counted, a legacy confirmed not only in the country's name, *Romania*, but also in its language (Latin, smudged) and expressions such as 'By Father Trajan', which could well have come down from the lost legions of Dacia.

I can find no evidence that Elena and Joe Słomnicki identified with the characters who grouped around Carol – 'a horrible set of low adventurers', according to his own mother – or the stage props of his reign, let alone felt any sympathy for the fast-accelerating blood-and-soil nationalism of Greater Romania, with its emphasis on racial superiority. On the contrary, everything about their lives at this point suggests they were invested in internationalism. Between them, they could speak and write in six languages, their living derived from the multinational cooperation of the oilfields, and their cultural outlook was just that: a looking out rather than in. It's not that my grandparents shunned a sense of belonging – I don't doubt their intention was to continue their life in Romania – but, even if they desired it, they didn't have the expectation of a life confirmed or delimited by a single national identity.

All these zigzags in the past can be of no interest to young children, because they live in the here and now, not the then and there. It's not that they don't have memory, it's that childhood is its own estate, free from the malady of history. So when a turn of the dial on Joe's new radio in the sitting room at Câmpina conjures up a man in Berlin who screams about historical injustices and lost lands,

Donald, six, and Peter, four, have no greater concern than what they're going to do today. Perhaps it's a Sunday, in which case there's Sunday School in Ploieşti run by a former army chaplain, Harold Chalmer Bell (he is also a people-smuggler, though he doesn't know it yet). This is conducted in English, which is confusing for Donald and Peter, who speak only German at home, though they will soon start to learn English with the aid of an au pair, Miss Weldon (on the day she arrived, Peter remembers, the boys rushed to show her the radio, turned the dial to the BBC and shrieked: 'Spik Inglish, Missie Weldon! Spik Inglish!'). Sunday School is fun because the Redgrave children are there and they all sing a few happy hymns, listen agog to Padre Bell's stories – he has a black beard and they believe he is a magician – and leave clutching a handful of stickers to put in their attendance books.

After Sunday School a treat, a trip to Bucharest to visit Kisslinger's stamp shop (open seven days a week, like much else in the capital), where Donald likes to spend his pocket money. They take the local train, which is probably late, unlike the Orient Express, which stops three times a week at Câmpina for two minutes before making its final run to Bucharest. Joe and Elena have been on this train, though always in the other direction, and the children – like everyone else in town – know the drill. The platform is swept, the geraniums and petunias are watered, the station-master brushes down his best tunic and glances at his chronometer, and spectators crowd onto every vantage point to catch sight of the first wisp of smoke.

The smell of arrival: varnish and axle grease. Attendants in chocolate-brown uniforms descend from the expensive carriages, painted dark blue with gold lettering, to help passengers aboard and guide them to their compartments, where they marvel at the intricate wooden panelling, the nickel knobs and fittings, the leather and the lacquer. Passengers lean out of the windows to buy walnuts and yoghurt. Vendors dash up and down the platform while engineers tap the wheels with long hammers. The guards mount the footboards, the doors are shut, handkerchiefs are waved, hats lifted, officials make the spectators draw back, the whistle is blown and the hiss of the engine drowns out all other sounds. The station is empty again, but for a few travellers waiting for a local train, which does not, alas, run with the same inflexibility of fate.

This train trundles along next to dusty country roads, oxen sauntering alongside, through fields of maize and sunflowers, past clusters of oil derricks and pumpjacks that peck the ground like giant birds. On the outskirts of Bucharest, there are lumber yards with freshly cut resinous logs piled high in blocks and slums with open drains where pockmarked children in bare feet play next to the tracks with hoops and jackstones. The journey takes about an hour and ends in the Gara de Nord which, like the streets beyond, is noisy with commerce. Trays heaped high with Turkish delight, to be chased down with cold spring water carried in wooden jugs and served from a metal cup on a chain clipped to the vendor's waist. Fifty *bani* for half a Turkish delight, one *leu* for a whole one. Shouts of '*Bragă racită, bragă racită!*' – cool millet beer, poured into glasses from a pump on the seller's back. On every pavement there are people selling garlicky black sausages dipped in red sauce, cups of steaming onion soup, yoghurt, sesame cakes, flowers and matches.

It's a short tram ride from the station to the corner of Strada Episcopiei at the junction with Bucharest's main boulevard, Calea Victoriei. Here stands the most elegant grand hotel of the Balkans, styled after the Meurice and the Ritz in Paris: the Athénée Palace, where members of the international press and various intriguers trade gossip for cocktails in the famous English Bar. Donald is already a veteran of the Athénée, having several times ridden the lift up and down with Roy Redgrave, who was born in a room on the second floor and therefore has special privileges, including visiting the kitchens to taste the *caracs*, small chocolate cakes covered in hard green icing. Joe and Elena sometimes come here for an aperitif (an Amalfi perhaps, the house combination of vermouth and *ţuică*) and a dollop of red caviar, before going to the Athenaeum for a concert – it might be George Enescu conducting one of his own compositions, or Artur Rubinstein playing Chopin – or to see a movie in one of the many cinemas that line Regina Elisabeta Boulevard.

Further down Calea Victoriei is the famous *confiserie*, Capsa's, with its pastries and gateaux, crystallised fruits, rose-petal jam and chocolates sold in wooden boxes with dovetail corners. There is also Dragomir's delicatessen, selling golden trout from the mountain streams, oranges from Jaffa, sturgeon six feet long, yellow honey, red caviar from Manchuria, hams from Prague and all the wines of Europe. Then there's the Lafayette department store with its wondrous window displays (at Christmas there is a Santa Claus standing in fake snow, and a train that keeps moving in a circle), and suddenly people crowd the pavements as a troop of mounted lancers in white uniforms come trotting down the boulevard. Donald and Peter beg to be lifted up for a glimpse of dazzling breastplates, lances, helmets streaming with plumes of white horse hair. Fun for the boys, but Joe, having spent three years in the field of war, will have noted that even the most glamorous uniform is little more than an imperfect casing for human offal.

Joe enters Lafayette with Peter while Elena proceeds to Kisslinger's on the other side of the boulevard. She grips Donald's hand tightly as they cross, dodging trams, automobiles, rattling carts, sheep, mangy dogs. Stamps being at the centre of his object world, Donald is immediately on tiptoe, scanning the glass display cases for the right stamp to complete a set. Elena waits patiently, her gaze drawn to the boulevard's belle-époque buildings and the *modernaki* not-quite-skyscraper opposite. The Paris of the East. Donald calls her over to show her a stamp. It's the man on the radio. She tells him he doesn't need to buy it, as he already has three of the same issue. (Here they are in his Kisslinger album: dark-green six-*pfennig* stamps bearing the first portrait of Adolf Hitler to appear on a German stamp, issued in April 1937 to celebrate his forty-eighth birthday. The pimp's forelock is carefully combed to one side.) Donald chooses something else, pays for his purchase and the shopkeeper throws the coins one by one on a flat stone on the counter to decide, by the ring of the impact, if they are counterfeit. Elena sighs impatiently. They don't do that in Paris.

They leave Kisslinger's and turn left onto the Calea Griviţei, heading to the Kodak shop to buy a roll of film for Joe's camera. The boulevard is heaving with passers-by, loafers, beggars, knots of peasants and vendors shouting their wares. Among this huge jostling are Albanians, Turks, Armenians, Bulgarians, Tartars, Russians, Germans, Hungarians, Poles, Greeks, Ruthenians, Ukrainians, Czechs, Slovaks, Jews and Roma. Paris recedes and the East comes closer. Elena, always nostalgic for another world, steps around the rinds of sucked-out watermelons, the crippled beggars with babies at their breasts, and wishes she could unsee this one.

THE STAMP ALBUMS

Hitler, Mussolini, George VI, Farouk I, Stalin, Roosevelt, Reza Shah, Ghazi, Hirohito, Atatürk, Zog, Horthy, Victor Emmanuel III, Leopold III, Haakon VII, Carol II, Peter II. Zeppelins, ships, aeroplanes, dams, bridges, mountains, eagles perching, eagles soaring, peasants threshing, workers smelting, surgeons stitching. Geniuses, madmen, heroes, villains – take your pick. History in miniature, light as air, a whisper, not a shout: this is the world we have made, admire it, admire us, even as we lie waxily in state or burn next to the bunker.

The albums also describe the collector. Thousands of stamps, hundreds of hours of inspection and ordering and careful handling: interleaving them in stock books with pockets of thin glassine paper; lifting out the best with tweezers, to be slotted into hinges or glued onto presentation pages; captioning each stamp or series in tiny script, underlined several times with a ruler. The precision of the line, the principle – the act – of order over the collapse of rule. Every time I look at these albums, I see the child who sits, deep in concentration, his legs curled around the rungs of his favourite chair (to every chair its own geography), trying to shape the world as he wants it to be.

It's as though what started as a hobby fast became a psychological necessity. Stamp collecting offered Donald a way to tame geography and fix boundaries. Surrounded as he was by adults who were not-from-here people, most of whom had been bullied by history in some way or other, I think he absorbed, from a very early age, the anxiety of displacement. Granny Helen, as I remember her, was a human *via dolorosa*: her face at rest was a study of unease and, even when smiling, she seemed tethered to unhappiness. Joe died the year I was born, so I never knew him, but in photographs he, too, looks as if life has taught him to baulk at contentment. The air around him seems heavy. I may be wrong, but I always had the suspicion that the dark regions of my father's mind, in which he was often recused, were an inherited estate.

As adults, mired in memory, we envy the innocence of childhood, forgetting that it is innocence that leaves the child undefended against the baffling, repeated affronts of daily life, each one landing out of nowhere like a hammer blow – the lost toy, the foisted vegetables *and you will not leave the table until you have eaten them*, the bedtime story curtailed, the light turned out. Gradually the child's developing sensorium organises these stunning events into a map of pain whose legend supplies the key to a less turbulent passage: the lost toy is usually found, the ice cream mitigates the *sauerkraut*, the bedtime story is resumed the following evening.

But beware, there be dragons – places you don't ever want to stray into. On his seventh birthday Donald was given an air rifle. He took it outside, aimed it at a bird sitting on a telegraph pole and fired. A pause, then the songbird dead at his feet, its fall describing the plummeting soul of its assassin, who still talked of his guilt half a century later. There were other shocks, each belonging to that shapeless and shifting suspicion, impossible to define, of something being innately wrong in the world: running out of the house one lunchtime as it was being wrestled by an earthquake, and returning to discover that part of the ceiling had fallen into his plate (Donald was keeping the best bits till last, a practice he immediately and permanently reversed); having his tonsils removed in a dentist's chair, only half-knocked out by a glass of brandy (a botched procedure, the tonsils were to reappear when he was fifteen); watching a scrawny bear waddling upright on a chain, a Turkish fez on its skull and a tambourine tied to one paw.

The story I've always told myself is that my father's childhood ended abruptly at the exact moment the gods chose to unload their discombobulations onto his innocent head, but I'm coming to see it more as a series of small shoves that hustled him, prematurely, across the boundary that was meant to protect him from too much contact with the sins of the world.

THREE

Nor can I find out the names of those who decided upon these boundaries or how the continents got their names.

Herodotus, *The Histories*, Book IV

A MEMORY OF my father spreading a map on the warm bonnet of the car, catching at its flapping corners in awkward gusts of Welsh wind. We are on a camping holiday, we are lost, and he is trying to tame the map so that we don't get loster. The high, solid hedgerows welded to the sides of the road obscure the view and are not marked on the map. Nor are the wild raspberries that grow in the hedgerow. Nor is the weather. Nor is the man spreading a map on the warm bonnet of the car, catching at its flapping corners in awkward gusts of Welsh wind.

My father was very fond of maps. He took great care to respect the original creases when folding them, and arranged them on dedicated bookshelves next to his impressive run of the *National Geographic*, whose bright-yellow spines I liked. I think he believed in maps at a very literal level, not simply as a reliable guide for getting from here to there, but as a set of agreed principles that give meaning to the world and tell us how it is. That this faith survived his youth, which was nothing if not a lesson in the treachery of maps, is a kind of miracle – a case of believing is seeing, rather than the other way round.

His faith was sometimes tested by discrepancies between the map and the territory, though it wasn't clear to me whether he believed the ground to be at fault or the map (that it might be the map-reader never entered the calculation). On one occasion, driving in Somerset to a church he wanted to see, me at the wheel, he holding the map, he became increasingly peeved that our destination was further away than he had expected. 'It's not where it should be,' he kept saying. We eventually found the church, which had a Norman nave and was therefore unlikely to have moved since the Ordnance Survey had landed its symbol on the Landranger map.

Thinking back on this, I wonder if my father was already in the early stages of dementia. He was only in his mid-fifties and it was a couple of years yet before it was plain to me that something was wrong. (This was when he left three identical messages on my answering machine, one after the other, informing me that his fax number had changed. I understood what this meant, and I sat down and burst into tears. It wasn't grief, as such, or even a rehearsal of grief; it was fear of the effort required to meet the situation. *You have three new messages.* I deleted them immediately.) On that drive in Somerset I had been surprised that he was so agitated: it was odd, disproportionate, but not enough to suggest that his cognitive functions were already compromised. It was as if, out of the corner of my eye, I had seen a few tiles blown off a roof (more awkward gusts of wind). I didn't recognise this as a warning that the ceiling of his brain was on the verge of collapse.

GEOGRAPHY LESSON PART ONE

It is said that the first lie of a map is that it tells the truth. The only true map would have to be on a scale of 1:1, a map that shows every single detail, including the map of the map of the map (keep repeating). Even supposing that such infinite regress could be shown (it can't), the map still wouldn't be truly true, because the territory itself can never be fixed – the map would have to be constantly altered, in real time, to include the fallen oak, the river that bursts its banks, the ooze of tarmac on the newly surfaced road. A map is a memory: it's a representation, a re-presenting – a bringing into, or returning to, the present – of something that has been. It may look good on paper (and that's already a fiddle, a projection of a sphere onto a plane), but it's always a botched job, and mapmakers know it. Hence a cartographic language loaded with confessions of omission and commission: *map silences, map fictions, map errors, distortion formulae (generalisation, adjustment, displacement, collapse), terra incognita.* Every map is a fiction, a *legend.* It is no more the territory than memory is the past.

Such considerations would not have been presented to the pupils of the local primary school in Câmpina, which Donald Słomnicki, then seven and speaking only a smattering of Romanian, attended from the autumn of 1938. Behind every teacher in every classroom in every school loomed a portrait of the king and a map of Greater Romania, the perfect circle within which, according to the curriculum and the powers-that-be, everybody lived happily cheek by jowl, doing various things in various states of traditional dress.

Here (the teacher prods the map with a ruler) are the marshlands of Dobruja, where the Ottomans fish and harvest reeds. Here in Braşov are the Saxon Germans of Transylvania, in their tight-fitting black gabardine suits and high boots, the same costume they wore when they arrived 200 years ago. Over here, in the upper valleys of the Mureş and Olt rivers, are the Szeklers; they are woodcutters and speak a dialect of Hungarian and some people say they are descended from Attila's Huns. And here are the flat steppes of the province of Bessarabia, which is very fertile, producing much of the country's food. Russia has colonised it several times, but it is and always will be ours.

Here, and here, and here are the sowing-reaping-threshing peasants, backbone of the nation. The men dress in light-green jackets braided with red or yellow, with large silver buttons hanging like bells, and they stuff their baggy trousers into top boots. The women wear smocks with colourful embroidered bodices, tucked into heavy pleated skirts that reach to the ground. The Dacian peasants of Transylvania, however, can be recognised by their long, loose shirts drawn in over the hips with a leather belt, heavy cloaks worn off the shoulders and, on their feet, sandals tied with cords or leather thongs – a costume virtually unchanged since their ancestors appeared on Trajan's Column.

And here (a long swoop of the arm from left to right) is the mighty River Danube, whose journey takes it from its source near the park of Sigmaringen, the home of the Hohenzollerns in the Black Forest, through Germany, Austria, Hungary and finally Yugoslavia, before it roars into Romania through the mighty Iron Gates. From this cauldron of gorges and cataracts, Romanian timber rolls all the way down to the yawning delta that flows into the Black Sea. The Iron Gates, where the Roman emperor Trajan engaged the Dacian tribes in battle and inflicted great losses, though not without taking some on his side (when the supply of bandages had given out, he cut his own clothes into strips). Trajan, believing he had conquered the Dacians, commemorated the victory on his column in Rome, which, as you all know, is in Italy. He also built a stone bridge across the Danube, east of the Iron Gates, to access his new forward positions, the *limes*, or limit, of the empire. The Via Pontica was an engineering marvel, but his successor, Emperor Hadrian, reasoning that a bridge goes two ways, took it down to prevent the barely subdued barbarians from crossing it.

Here is the great capital of Greater Romania, *Bucureşti*, founded a long, long time ago by a shepherd named Bucur. It is very beautiful, this Paris of the East. Just above *Bucureşti* we find the Prahova valley, the centre of our biggest industry, oil. The oil-bearing strata extend north-eastwards to Focşani, here, and westwards towards Craiova, here. Câmpina, our town, is also rich in oil and it has two cinemas. End of lesson. *Traiasca Romania Mare*, Long Live Greater Romania.

Finally, after school, here is home in all its familiarity, its comfortably small geography offsetting the classroom rigour of thinking big. The gate that opens inwards (you have to push hard when it's been raining), the garden with the climbing pole and swing, both of which seem to get smaller every year, the door handle that turns left not right, the hook on which you sling your satchel, the slash of light in the hallway, the changing sound as you pass from stone to wooden floors (the warm spot underfoot where a pipe runs), the creak in the stair, the clang of hot water coming out of the tap, the warm, patterned tiles of the ceramic stove, the weave and heft and warp and weft that tell you where you stand in the greater scheme of things.

In the sitting room the man on the radio who screeches on and on from Berlin doesn't like the map that tells him where he stands; he wants to change it so that he has more room. That's why Austria doesn't exist any more and Czechoslovakia has got smaller. Czechoslovakia has a border with Romania and everybody is worried that the man on the radio is going to cross it with his Panzer tanks so that he can continue eastwards to make one really big, joined-up 'living space'. In Vienna, they say, many shops are displaying three maps showing what this will look like: the first map is titled 'THE GERMANY WHICH WAS', the second 'THE GERMANY WHICH IS' and the third 'THE GERMANY WHICH WILL BE'.

Bulgaria, Hungary and Soviet Russia also want to change the map. They claim that Romania stole chunks of their countries and should give them back. This can be done by redrawing a few red lines on the map, after which the Bulgarians, Hungarians and Russians will have returned home without actually moving. 'Revisionism', the adults call it, though not in front of the children, because how do you explain the undoing of geography without mentioning that people like us could find ourselves living in the wrong map, the map where the bodies pile up?

Much better to concentrate their minds on the exciting futuristic constructions that are popping up at border zones everywhere, especially the Maginot Line in France, 'the greatest defensive system ever devised'. Joe has a subscription to the *Illustrated London News* – his collection of back-issues dating to the 1920s is handsomely bound in red leather volumes – and it has photographs and artists' impressions of France's fortifications along its eastern border with Germany. Donald and Peter are not yet proficient enough in English to understand the text, so Joe translates into German as they go along:

The essential points of the French system, which was carried out on a gigantic scale, are as follows: a line of fortified casemates giving each other mutual protection by cross-fire, and interconnected by underground galleries safe from bombardment. All the key positions, normally vulnerable to aerial and other attack, are buried underground, such as living-quarters, magazines, stores, power-stations and control posts.

This vast subterranean adventure playground is illustrated with a double-spread 'diagrammatic drawing'. It is a world within a world, a Jules Verne world – what fun grown-ups have.

'*Nous sommes imprenables.*' Nobody shall pass. The line is 'unassailable', 'invulnerable', 'formidable', 'impregnable'. So clever, in fact, that it 'has set a fashion followed all over Europe, by Belgium, Russia, Switzerland and Poland. But the greatest imitator of all is Germany, which has now tried to checkmate the Maginot Line by fortifications on the German side.' This is the *Westwall*, but in English it is known as the Siegfried Line. It was started by Hitler under cover of an archaeological excavation of the ancient Roman *limes*, but it's no longer a secret and appears regularly in Nazi propaganda films, which are carefully edited to obscure the fact that it is not as complete as it seems to be.

King Carol II, the Great and the Good, Father of Culture, Father of his People, is also busy organising a system of defence to match his pledge that 'Not one foot of Romanian territory shall pass into the hands of our enemies.' He has been touring the country, making speeches to rally his subjects to the task of building a great moat, thirty-six feet deep, on the border with Soviet Russia. Running parallel with the River Dniester, from the Carpathians to the Black Sea, this dyke – once oil is pumped into it and ignited – will become 'a wall of liquid fire'. Soon, the Carol Line will form an unbroken chain of fortifications, 'a living wall against aggression'.

'"RIVERS OF FIRE" TO GUARD RUMANIA: CANALS TO BE FILLED WITH OIL, CONCRETE AND BARBED WIRE,' reads the headline above the *Illustrated London News*'s spread on 'Romania's Own Maginot Line'. At first glance, and second, the photographs are not quite as convincing as the king's pronouncements. One shows the reinforcement of the Bessarabian frontier with the Soviet Union, consisting of 'horizon-wide plains dissected by' – rather thin – 'belts of barbed wire, which are also mined'; another shows a 'section of a concrete wall' – two slabs (are there any more?) – 'joined with iron barriers which in case of need can be electrified'; in another, a handful of men, barefoot and with their trousers rolled up, or with no trousers at all, use shovels to widen a canal, passing the mud back along the line to be piled up into a berm that looks like a landslip-in-waiting.

A photograph of the adjacent Bukovina front features a single mechanical excavator digging a canal, 'which might' – *might?* – 'become a "river of fire" hundreds of miles long'. The bucket of the digger, which swings precariously from an improvised rig, is shown scooping mud out of the canal, most of which seems to be falling back into the water; its operator has casually thrown his jacket on the ground beside it, and presumably any minute now he will be stopping for lunch. Last, a photograph of Romanian soldiers in bearskin hats, bearing antique-shop carbines with fixed bayonets, 'prepared to defend the integrity of their country inch by inch' from behind 'high protective barricades', which look no sturdier than cold frames for growing cucumbers.

All along the Carol Line, tens of thousands of conscripts, many of them still without uniforms, cringe before the blasts of the *crivăţ*, the wind from the steppes that announces the Balkan winter. They stand at their posts, stamping from one foot to the other, hands in their sleeves. The mounted officers, too, are cold, despite stuffing newspaper under their greatcoats and into their boots. Occasionally a group of them arrives to inspect the line and exhort the conscripts, *sons of the people*, to protect this holy Romanian soil from invaders. Together with the local inhabitants, they all peer across the no-man's-land beyond and wonder if war will really be coming here:

> *They creep from their huts, our people, swarming towards us to greet us, bring ţuică – mild, oily plum brandy – and delicately rancid cakes: a people smelling rancid in their sheepskins, with deeply notched peasant faces, children peeping timidly from behind their mothers' aprons, silver-haired old men, trembling, dribbling, with broken voices, and here and there the cherry-dark eyes of a girl, the double humps of firm breasts under an embroidered blouse ... people who have grown out of their soil, with hair like grass, with skin like bark, with hands like tree roots – and young girls plump as cherries. And we among them in our uniforms and helmets, warriors hung with sabres, lances, and carbines, with our hoary, steam-breathing horses – it all looks like an opera set.*

The Imaginot Line, people call it, under their breath. In the cafés of Bucharest 'waiters bring ball-shaped chocolate cakes pimpled over like naval mines' (Siegfrieds, or Maginots, depending on the waiter's best guess as to the nationality of his clients).

It took twenty-four hours to take Austria off the map. German troops crossed the border on 12 March 1938, and the next day the occupation of Adolf Hitler's country of birth was complete. 'Swarms of Berlin League of German Maiden girls have been directed here for the moment, and they wave ecstatically at the tank columns rattling through the streets. In the next issue of the *Berliner Illustrierte Zeitung* they will be pictured as "Local Inhabitants, Who Greeted Their Liberators with Wild Ovations".' This, one eye-witness confided to his diary, was a piece of stagecraft devised by Goebbels, 'the limping haberdashery salesman', to camouflage the political burglary that was taking place. Three days later the burglar-in-chief rode into Vienna in an open Mercedes, lifting and lowering his right arm while his left hand 'held tight to his belt buckle, as though he were afraid that his pants might fall down'. This being the age of balcony politics, Hitler appeared on one to announce the *Anschluss*, the 'joining' of Austria to the Fatherland, a process speedily confirmed by a plebiscite in which the great majority of Austrians consciously voted away the independence of their country. *Heim ins Reich* – 'Back home to the Reich'.

When corresponding with friends and relatives in Vienna, say, or Salzburg, Donald's mother, Elena, now had to address her letters to Germany. As the Austrian postal service no longer existed, letters posted from the new territory of *Ostmark* (Eastern March) had to use German stamps, and there being no Austrian currency any more, they had to be purchased in German *Reichspfennig*. The stamp issued in April 1938 to celebrate the *Anschluss* pictured two men in fraternal embrace waving a swastika flag, who were themselves embraced by the script *Ein Volk – Ein Reich – Ein Führer*. There were to be no more Austrian stamps until November 1945.

It's impossible to know whether Donald understood the reason for the sudden disappearance of stamps from the country previously known as Österreich. (I'm sure he noticed: he had a good collection of Austrian stamps up to this point, and every stamp collector has a greedy eye for what is not there.) As Elena was ethnically German, she may have had some difficulty explaining this development to herself, let alone to her small boys. After all, Herr Hitler was at the service of her manifest destiny, working to restore her to her proper home in Grossdeutschland, a project that had been worming through his mind ever since he was sleeping on park benches in Vienna, a failed artist too hard up to consume anything other than the German nationalism of local firebrands. Never mind Elena's previous or current nationality, nothing could obscure the fact that, in Hitler's estimation, she belonged by blood to Greater Germany.

Blut und Boden, blood and soil: the doctrine of racial belonging in which nature is suborned to the claims of unreality, so that there can be such a thing as *German* blood, *German* soil. It is not a metaphor, it is understood to be literally true that if you pick up a handful of soil in Germany, it really *is* German, different somehow from the soil fifty yards away across the border; and that if you are German, then so is your blood, which, when pricked, will show itself to be vastly superior to anybody else's blood.

Other nations were to take up this nonsense with more or less murderous results, but none as industriously as Nazi Germany. For Hitler, here was the biogeographical alibi for his policy of *Lebensraum*, or 'living space.' As to how 115 million ethnic Germans (according to him) living in Central and Eastern Europe would be reunited with/restored to the *Vaterland*, Hitler favoured the principle of returning an omelette to an egg. This would involve the unmixing of peoples and the careful removal of any elements not fit for inclusion – Jews, Poles, homosexuals, communists, socialists, Roma, Jehovah's Witnesses, Slavs, Roman Catholics, pacifists, Freemasons, Esperantists. To achieve this, every territory containing blood-Germans, even if they had been there for centuries and didn't speak a word of German, needed to be occupied and annexed to the Reich.

As our diarist put it, 'every nation normally puts its demons, its delusions, its impossible desires away into the cellars and vaults and underground prisons of its unconscious; the Germans have reversed the process, and have let them loose. The contents have escaped like the winds out of Pandora's box.'

At the Versailles Conference in 1919, Queen Marie had 'shuddered' to think of the possible repercussions of the 'ghastly' peace terms being forced on Germany. 'I thought of the hideous suffering which would follow, of the seething hatred which would make many million hearts fester with an undying desire of future revenge ... I could not help feeling that it was unwise to go so far – too far.' She did not extend the insight to her own country, whose greatness had been gifted by that same peace. Dying on 18 July 1938, shortly after the *Anschluss*, she was spared the sight of Greater Romania vomiting up its gains.

Her state funeral in Bucharest drew a quarter of a million people. The coffin, draped in mauve and covered with her standard, was carried out of the royal palace (much of which was still a building site) by officers of her beloved regiment, the Rosciori, and placed on a gun carriage drawn by six black horses. A salute of seventy-five guns was fired, aeroplanes roared overhead, church bells tolled as the cortège made its way through the packed boulevards to Mogoşoaia station, from where the coffin was transported by train to the cathedral of Curtea de Argeş, north-west of Bucharest. With thousands of people holding candles lining the railway track, it took the train six hours to make a two-hour journey. In a private ceremony, Marie was interred that evening next to her husband, who had died in 1927. Her heart, as she had desired, was taken to her summer home at Balchik on the Black Sea Coast and installed in the chapel there.

Very likely, Joe and Elena went to Bucharest to pay their respects to the late queen, though I doubt they would have taken the children, for fear of being separated in the crowd. It was not to spare them an encounter with death, for they had already had this. Elena's father, Ernst, had died two years earlier, in 1936, and the boys had visited him on his deathbed, though Peter remembers only that he stood by a bed so high he couldn't see who was in it.

For the Hottis, like the Hohenzollerns, death was something to be organised around dignity, restraint and the laws of established religion. They did not do it the Romanian way, which had its own irrepressible idiom. Death was openly confessed, with most of the population being taken for burial in open coffins or no coffin at all. It was an event to be faced, not denied – people who knew they were dying often prepared their own burial clothes – and was accompanied by a host of archaic rites whose origins were frequently a mystery, and all the better for that. Superstition doesn't generally pin its colours to reason, and in Romania mystification was its own kind of belief – hardly surprising in a land that had been settled and squabbled over by Greeks, Romans, Celts, Tartars and Scythian Huns, Vandals and Goths, Magyars, Avars, Slavs, Ottomans, Mongols, Dravidians, not to mention those early humans of thirty-five millennia ago whose footprints were discovered in a cave in the Carpathians. In Romania, a thousand years is no time at all.

The process of dying and the journey into the afterlife was minutely mapped. First came the omens of death: unexpected cracking or creaking of tables or chairs, things falling off the walls (mirrors, icons), a hen crowing like a cock, a dog howling or, worst of all, an owl calling. If the death-throes were prolonged and agonising, the person doing the dying was placed on the ground, face to the east and with eyes closed, to spare him or her witnessing the sorrow and pain of relatives.

After death, all mirrors and clocks in the home were turned to the wall, and windows and doors were opened to give the soul an easy exit – to which end, pails of water were covered to prevent it from falling in and drowning. If the head of the family had died, the oxen were harnessed with the harness upside-down, symbolising the topsy-turviness of the situation. The body was washed and vigil kept over it for two days and nights to prevent the Devil from snatching it; female relatives and professional mourners performed the *bochirea*, or lament, three times a day, taking care not to let their tears fall on the face of the corpse, lest they burn or drown its innocent soul.

On the third day a coin was placed in the dead person's hand, to pay for the boatman to row across the River Styx, and the body was put into an open coffin or, just as commonly, onto the unhinged front door of the house, then loaded onto a two-wheeled cart and slowly trundled or drawn to the cemetery. As the coffin was lowered into the grave, mourners poured red wine, grains of wheat and coins over it and, lastly, a handful of earth, thereby forgiving all the slights committed by the deceased against them. Then the mourners went home – taking care to return by a different route – for the rowdy *Praznik*, or funeral supper.

Donald was surely familiar with the noisier, hard-to-avoid elements of the Romanian way of death. He may even have witnessed corpses emerging feet-first on their own front doors. I don't know if this would have frightened him or simply piqued his curiosity. Children, like the dead, can be very cold-blooded. That said, I was never equipped with this sangfroid. My maternal grandfather died when I was ten, and I thought he more or less deserved it, because he had short-changed me (on the only occasion he actually spoke to us, as I recall it, he had given my brother two fifty-pence pieces and me two ten-pence pieces). So I surprised myself at his funeral by crying uncontrollably, to the point where I nearly had to be carried out. It set a stubborn precedent: of all the forms of energetic stupidity I am prone to, this overblown behaviour at funerals is the one I am most ashamed of. Obviously I have a problem with death.

The *Anschluss* and, soon afterwards, the 'reoccupation' of the Sudetenland to 'liberate' the 'poor, persecuted, oppressed German minority' announced the era of smash-and-grab, of brute intruders unable to resist the possessions of others. (Felicitations: Hitler's Czechoslovakian smash-and-grab yielded the Skoda works at Pilsen, the largest armament works in the world.) It follows that this was also the era of hiding things, of sewing jewels and currency into the seams of coats, of stowing belongings under floorboards or digging them into the earth, of concealing the colour of your hair (self-Aryanisation by peroxide, as long as supplies lasted), of burying your feelings lest they betray you.

Donald's best friend, Roy Redgrave, discovered that his father kept a loaded .45 service revolver hidden under his bedside table. Roy knew his father as 'a happy-go-lucky man', so why did he feel threatened in his own home? Roy, now thirteen, was attending a boarding school in England, travelling back and forth on his own on the Orient Express, which used to be fun, but wasn't any more. Officials were no longer polite or friendly; border guards appeared in different uniforms at every frontier crossing, demanding passengers' documents and searching their baggage. When the train stopped at Vienna, men in black uniforms and jackboots, with the skull-and-crossbones badge on their caps, stalked the compartments and took some people off the train. Jews, it was murmured. The fear had always been that the Orient Express, this civilised conveyance of European values, was under threat from the barbarians and brigands of the uncivilised East. Now it was the reverse.

Also journeying to Vienna on the Orient Express at this time was the wealthy son of a baronet, who happens to be a great-great-uncle on my mother's side. I bumped into this coincidence while searching the archive of *The Times* for news of the *Anschluss*, only to find a letter to the editor, dated 2 April 1938, from the Hon. Edward Stonor. Improbable as it sounds, Edward was hoping for some game-shooting in Austria and saw no reason for German field artillery to deflect his plan. 'At Buchs, on the Swiss-Austrian frontier,' he writes:

> *we were invaded by six or seven very young Nazi officials, who took stock of our money and pored over our passports ... I was bringing with me for a friend two English sporting guns, and these caused much speculation among the Nazi officials, who wanted to know the military value of such guns. I assured them that over 100 yards they were of no military value, and were intended solely for game destruction.*

This seemed to satisfy the Nazis, and Edward, along with only five other passengers, was allowed to proceed in his luxury capsule through a landscape 'dotted with the long red streamers of Nazidom' (at St Anton, he noticed, even the station dog was wearing a swastika). The train passed Innsbruck, Salzburg, Linz, Wels – everywhere the bloody surge of flags – and finally arrived in Vienna, where troops marched down the Ringstrasse as German planes flew in formation overhead. Hitler's portrait was displayed in all the shop windows of Kärntnerstrasse, 'the Bond Street of Vienna', and every other shop was signed with the letters NSBO (*Nazional Sozialistische Betriebszellen Organisation*, or National Socialist Enterprise Organisation), which meant that it was 'cleansed' of the Jewish taint and was now run by Aryans.

Edward arrived at his hotel, the Bristol, where he had stayed many times before, to find that it, too, was NSBO and its 'genial manager [had] been superseded'; he went to the Rothschild Bank in Renngasse (currency restrictions having left him short of cash), but its doors were closed and 'the head of the house and its chief cashier in prison'. The most startling sight, he reported, was 'the vast crowd struggling to get into the British Consulate in the Wallnerstrasse', which filled the staircase and overflowed into the street. Jews, desperately trying to get visas. 'Poor, demented folk, they had little chance of success,' Edward correctly predicted. 'One wonders what the future holds in store for [them], except starvation.' There was one sure way out, he soon discovered. An 'epidemic' of suicide had swept the city: 'in an unconsecrated corner near the great Central Cemetery I saw the newly dug graves of many Lebensmüde, who by their own hands had sought that rest which was denied to them in life'.

The British were not yet minded to save Jews, although they would take a small number of them as servants. One enterprising man (the purged manager of the Bristol Hotel?) opened a butlers' school on the Praterstrasse, where Jewish bankers and intellectuals were taught how to wait on the British. 'I once went there with Minka, and we laughed our heads off,' says the anti-Semitic narrator of Gregor von Rezzori's short story, 'Troth'. 'Old stockbrokers were waddling around with aprons about their hips, balancing trays and opening bottles of champagne.'

We find the de-classed Jews of Austria seeking sanctuary in the Public Appointments section of the classified pages of *The Times*. See under: COMPANIONS AND GOVERNESSES, PARLOURMAIDS AND HOUSE-PARLOURMAIDS, HOUSEMAIDS, MANSERVANTS, GARDENERS, LADY GARDENERS, HOUSE-KEEPERS, LADIES' MAIDS AND MAIDS, BETWEENMAIDS AND GENERALS, MARRIED COUPLES AND MANSERVANTS, CHAUF-FEURS, CHAUFFEUSES.

11 May 1938: *Young, well-educated Viennese Nursery Governess, pleasant appearance, desires post: mother tongue German, good command of English; experienced in kindergarten and domestic work, plain cooking, first-class references – Write to Lisel Braun, Arenbergring 10, Vienna III.*

23 May 1938: *Housekeeper or Companion-Help. Austrian lady, age 40, good birth and education, seeks post: good cook, needlewoman, fluent English, French; pianist; willing to care for children; highest credentials. Write Box 4435, Frost-Smith Advertising, London EC2.*

27 May 1938: *Young Austrian lady (Jewish) seeks position Governess; experienced; good references; teaches German, French, Italian; would accept modest salary; good family. Write Box T.1653, The Times, EC4.*

6 June 1938: *Mechanic, 23, Jew, one year off diploma, seeks job as Constructor – Armin Freudmann, Vienna, IX Glasergasse 19.*

20 June 1938: *Well-educated young Austrian (25 years), smart appearance, of excellent Jewish family, seeks post as Chauffeur, Gentleman Servant, &c.: well informed in automechanics – Franz Leeb, Vienna XIV, Pillergasse 5.*

4 July 1938: *Very efficient Viennese Cook (non-Aryan) of good family seeks position as Housekeeper; 17-year-old daughter seeks position as Nursemaid; both experienced in all household duties. Friedlander, 44 Weissegarberlinde, Vienna III.*

4 July 1938: *Correspondent for English, German, French, and Italian – Austrian lawyer, Jew, perfect typist, wants a position – Dr Robert Fischer, Deutsch-mesiterplatz 2, Vienna I.*

28 July 1938: *Young Jewess, opera and concert singer, music teacher, Vienna Music Academy with honours, besides well-trained doctor's assistant, speaking French, Italian, German, perfect household duties, wants any occupation. Apply under 'Aged 28', care of Advertising Office, Emil Hirsch, 12 Kartnerring, Vienna I.*

28 July 1938: *Despairing Austrian couple with two children (boy aged 8, girl aged 1½ year) obliged to leave Vienna, seek work in England, Colonies, or Dominions; without resources or relatives abroad; husband bookkeeper, managing director of Viennese Fair, speaks English fluently; wife excellent housekeeper and splendid cook; content with smallest post enabling them to keep their children from starving – Kindly write to Mrs E. Stossl, Vienna II, Ferdinandstrasse 22, Germany.*

What happened to you, Lisel Braun? Mrs E. Stossl, with your husband and two children? Mrs Friedlander? Franz Leeb? Did you manage to get out?

Armin Freudmann, were you the Israel Armin Freudmann, born 1915, of 'no profession', who was deported from Vienna to Belgium and taken from there, as prisoner number 547 on Transport 13, 10 October 1942, to Auschwitz Birkenau Extermination Camp, where you were murdered? Or was this another Armin Freudmann from Vienna of exactly your age?

Dr Robert Fischer, did you make it to England with your typewriter? Or was it you who was deported from Vienna to Buchenwald Extermination Camp in Germany, to be murdered there on 18 July 1940?

Or were you the Robert Fischer who was deported from Vienna on 26 February 1941, Transport 3, prisoner number 3, to Opole Lubelskie, Lublin, Poland, to be murdered there?

Or the Robert Fischer deported on 19 October 1941 from Vienna on Transport 7, Train 5, prisoner number 372, to the Łódź Ghetto, Poland, to be murdered there?

Or was it you who was deported from Vienna on 16 June 1942 to Izbica in Poland, and then to Treblinka Extermination Camp to be murdered there?

Or were you the Robert Fischer deported from Vienna to Auschwitz Extermination Camp, Poland, 12 October 1942, to be murdered there?

Or the Robert Fischer deported on Transport 24, Train 205, prisoner number 821, from Vienna to Minsk, Belorussia, 2 June 1942, to be murdered at Maly Trostenets Camp?

Or the Robert Fischer deported from Vienna a week later, 9 June 1942, on Transport 26, Train 206, prisoner number 701, to Minsk, Belorussia, to be murdered at Maly Trostenets Camp on 15 June 1942?

Or the Robert Fischer deported from Vienna on 17 July 1942, Transport 32, Train 69, prisoner number 616, to Auschwitz-Birkenau Extermination Camp, Poland, to be murdered there?

Or were you the Robert Fischer deported from Vienna on 20 August 1942, Transport 37, Train 504, prisoner number 806, to Theresienstadt Ghetto, Czechoslovakia, to be murdered there on 6 June 1944?

GEOGRAPHY LESSON PART TWO

Hitler, who liked to be photographed studying maps, understood that the physical and human world can be mapped according to almost any principle. His chosen cartographic method was to go back in order to go forward: to explain the lie of the land (and it *was* a lie) by promoting a vision of how it used to be; and then to encourage the belief that this historical 'reality', despite the assaults of time, could be reinstated in the future. Hence the maps that Edward Stonor saw widely displayed following the *Anschluss*, with their three separate but contiguous views of the 'Germany that was', the 'Germany that is' and the 'Germany that will be'.

Hitler's retrospective gaze was Homerically expansive, even taking in the claim that the ancient Greeks were actually Germans 'who had survived a northern natural catastrophe and evolved a highly developed culture in southern contexts' – a preposterous fantasy, but worth pursuing for those archaeologists who coveted tenure in the now generously funded subject of 'Germanic prehistory'. In support of this project of creating a better yesterday, the entire intellectual vocabulary of German archaeology was changed. In 1935 the prehistoric and early historical chronologies were officially renamed: the Bronze and pre-Roman Iron Ages became the 'Early Germanic period', the Roman Iron Age the 'Climax Germanic period', the Migration period the 'Late Germanic period,' and everything from the Carolingians to the thirteenth century the 'German Middle Ages'.

Heinrich Himmler, who was obsessed with Germanic runes (the double lightning bolt, symbol of the SS, was adapted from one), took charge of surveying this holistic, supranational past, and soon maps of Neolithic culture in Europe spreading from a Germanic homeland began to proliferate in popular magazines and films. Poland, for example, was shown as part of 'The German Ostmark, Home Territory of the Germans'. Once it had been established, on the (fraudulent) basis of the distribution of archaeological remains, that there had been an original *Lebensraum*, restoring it to its rightful owners was axiomatic. Centuries of indignity, culminating in the Treaty of Versailles, could now be 'rectified' by removing the peoples – Slavic, Jewish or any other biological faux pas – who occupied what had once been Germanic territory. It would fall to Germany to inherit the earth because everybody else was squatting.

Hitler knew that the Greeks-were-really-Germans story was bunk, and much else besides. 'Why do we call the whole world's attention to the fact that we have no past?' he once complained to Albert Speer.

It's bad enough that the Romans were erecting great buildings when our forefathers were still living in mud huts; now Himmler is starting to dig up these villages of mud huts and enthusing over every potsherd and stone axe he finds. All we prove by that is that we were still throwing stone hatchets and crouching around open fires when Greece and Rome had already reached the highest stage of culture.

Himmler, Reich Commissioner for the Strengthening of Germandom, didn't believe it either, but that wasn't the point. As he explained it, 'The one and only thing that matters to us is to have ideas of history that strengthen our people in their necessary national pride. We are only interested in one thing – to project into the dim and distant past the picture of our nation as we envisage it for the future.'

The Germany that will be: geography overlaid with geomancy. When the world is mapped as a predictive phenomenon, every location, every boundary, is a potential zone of change. If every place can be *re*-placed, or *dis*-placed, then no place is safe.

It was still possible, in the summer of 1939, to imagine that everything would blow over. Not because events supported this hope, but because reality, once it becomes unreal, provides for all sorts of illusions. 'Intense wish fantasy', Freud would call it, even as he failed to recognise as such his own belief in the possibility of continuing to live in Vienna after the *Anschluss*, even as the Nazis draped a swastika over the entrance of his office and home at Berggasse 19.

As Roy Redgrave recalled it, that 'last summer' was memorable for its flight from reality. The Redgraves stayed in the villa of their exiled friend, Prince Ştirbei, in the Black Sea resort of Constanţa. The villa, complete with minaret, sat beside the golden sands of Mamaia beach, overlooking Ovid's Island on whose tiny surface the poet was said to have spun out his letters of exile 2,000 years earlier. 'My father made sure we never had a dull moment,' writes Roy. 'The tension building up in Europe was forgotten and I do not believe he or any of the many friends who visited us listened to the radio or read a newspaper during those last three idyllic weeks of August 1939.'

Joe and Elena and the children were among those who visited. If I'm right that the photographs in one of the family albums were taken on that holiday, then the atmosphere does indeed seem to have been genuinely carefree.

Perhaps they really did allow themselves to believe the faithfully repeated Allied blah that Hitler had missed the bus; that the Maginot Line was impenetrable; that there would be 'peace in our time'. Perhaps they all strolled over to see the Navy Day celebrations in Constanța on 15 August, attended by King Carol, looking suntanned in his white uniform after sailing the Mediterranean on his yacht; and perhaps they drifted away for an ice cream just as his speech embarked on the warning that those who loved peace should know that frontiers, once drawn, cannot be changed without danger of a world cataclysm.

We could try to agree, even, that they silently connived in not hearing the news, announced on 23 August, that Germany and the Soviet Union had agreed a non-aggression pact – a violent swerve that caused panic all over Europe and left Romania sandwiched between two powers that, in concert, could not possibly be resisted – but I think that's a stretch too far. It's not as if Constanța was on a different planet, even if Ovid had thought so. Either the adults hid their alarm from the children, or, equally possible, they continued with the holiday-from-the-truth charade because it was the only escape from the flood of dread released by the king from his podium on the beach.

Cataclysm. It came the day after the summer holiday ended, just before dawn on 1 September 1939, when German tanks crunched into Poland from the north, south and west. Two days later the Redgrave family stood in silence around the tall mahogany radio in the sitting room at Doftana to hear Neville Chamberlain's declaration on the BBC that Great Britain and Germany were at war. Joe and Elena may have been with them or they may have listened on their own radio in Câmpina – what difference does it make, except to say that listening to the BBC would soon be a crime in Romania?

A week later Roy and his sisters leaned on their Opel bicycles and watched a seemingly endless tide of human wreckage as it streamed along the main road outside Câmpina:

They were Polish refugees, exhausted old men, women and children, pushing prams, handcarts and bicycles, leading a cow or a goat, riding on farm carts piled high with bundles of bedding and household effects. There were motorcars with battered sides, broken headlights and mattresses tied to the roofs, all crammed with grey faces. There were smart carriages with huddled figures in fur coats drawn by tired horses whose heads hung low and a few Polish soldiers who trudged past in mud-stained uniforms, conspicuous in their distinctive diamond-shaped caps.

It was 'a shattering sight', and the Redgrave children were unable to speak to each other. When they got home, their father told them he had seen the sides of Bucharest airfield lined with battered Polish warplanes.

Roy was no longer treated as a child by his parents (nor by Florica, a housemaid who had secretly introduced him to fornication just short of his twelfth birthday). He was now fourteen, a seasoned traveller on the Orient Express, which took him, unaccompanied, to and from boarding school in England. Five years older than Donald, Roy had become his intermediary to the world at large – a role that continued, in some degree, for the span of their lifelong friendship. He brought news on subjects ranging from the full English breakfast to the London trains that ran under the ground, and no doubt it was Roy, rather than Joe or Elena, who kept Donald informed about the very bad thing that was happening in Poland.

Initially, Romania attempted to limit the number of Polish refugees entering the country, especially the Jews of Galicia. But on 21 September, following Stalin's invasion of Poland from the east, Russian tanks had reached the border town of Zaleszczyki, on the River Dniester, just as it was being ruthlessly bombed by the Germans. With a huge mass of desperate people gathering on the bridge, Romanian border guards removed all passport controls and lifted the barrier on their side. Nobody ran – there were too many people. They just shuffled across in penguin steps. Behind them, and benefiting from a radiantly clear day, German planes swooped low to strafe a twenty-mile bottleneck of refugees.

Those who had made it into Romania plugged doggedly along roads and dirt tracks, chivvied by local police who had no idea in which direction to send them. Many had not eaten for days; they would fall out of the straggling line to eat the seeds of sunflowers from the nearby fields. Bewildered locals came out to watch the sorry procession, took pity, offered food and water, a place to rest. Most of the refugees headed south, the only reason being that it was opposite to north, whence they had come.

Going in the other direction were tens of thousands of conscripted Romanians, surging up to the frontier to reinforce the border. Most of them were peasants, still in the clothes they were wearing in the fields when the summons came. They set off with little more than their *mămăliga* and their onions rolled up in a small parcel, to lug stones and dig trenches in Bessarabia. 'No enemy will ever be able to trample what is sacredly and eternally Romanian,' the king had told them, mystically. So off they went, no questions asked.

Roy had hoped that the crisis enveloping Europe would prevent his return to Sherborne School, so it was a bitter disappointment to learn that he would be leaving by train from Câmpina on the Simplon-Orient Express,* via Yugoslavia and Italy (Mussolini having yet to enter the war on Hitler's side). There was a tearful farewell on the platform, his mother slipped a small icon into his pocket, his father hugged him, his sisters wailed, the train drew off and, after endless delays, a week later Roy arrived in London. There, a family friend gave him half a crown, a cup of tea and a digestive biscuit, before sending him off to catch a train to Sherborne from Waterloo station. That night in the dormitory, he felt under his pillow for his icon and cried himself to sleep. He would not see any of his family again for six years.

Had Roy been able to delay his departure by even one day, he might have avoided this wrenching separation and the estrangement that followed. As it was, his train had already left Romanian territory by the time the king declared a national emergency and ordered that every frontier be closed immediately. Telephone lines went dead, cavalry and infantry armed with machine guns were drafted into Bucharest and larger towns, while armed police set up roadblocks to search all vehicles and pedestrians.

This was on 21 September 1939, the day when German and Soviet forces were laying waste to Zaleszczyki in Poland, but the two events were unrelated. That afternoon the Romanian prime minister, Armand Călinescu, had been assassinated in Bucharest. As his official car approached the Elefterie bridge, a group of Iron Guardists, a fascist militia also known as the Greenshirts (brown having already gone to the Nazis, black to the Italian *Fascisti*, and blue to the exuberantly anti-Semitic Romanian National

---

* The Orient Express was not, as many still suppose, a train, but a service, a network of routes using different rolling stock. By September 1939 the Orient Express and Nord Express routes to the Channel ports had been suspended.

Christian Party), came out from their hiding place under a timber cart and opened fire. Călinescu took seventeen bullets and died on the spot, as did his bodyguard. His assassins then stormed the national radio station, where they announced their heroic action, unaware that nobody could hear it because transmission had already been interrupted by radio staff. When the police arrived twenty minutes later, they gave themselves up and were taken to the *Prefectura* (police headquarters) for interrogation, which, as all parties knew, would involve a well-honed pattern of escalating torture.

By the time they were driven back to the scene of the crime the following evening, the assassins could barely stand. Under the glare of powerful arc lights installed for the purpose, and a placard that read 'Traitors to the country!' they were propped up and machine-gunned in front of a large crowd. Their twisted bodies were left on the pavement for twenty-four hours, surrounded by reservists whose job it was to control the thousands of people who arrived by tram, by bus or on foot to take in the sight. 'It was like a big fair,' wrote one eye-witness:

> They were laughing and joking. Those who were unable to squeeze through to the front saw nothing. A lady beside me said: 'They should keep order, put us in two rows so that everyone can see.' People from nearby had brought some wooden stepladders, and those who wanted a better view paid two lei to climb up and look over the rest. 'Don't do it!' said one guy who had paid his two lei but had been disappointed. 'Don't do it! All you can see are their feet.'

The corpses were then taken to Ploieşti to hang from lamp posts, again drawing spectators, this time organised into a queue so that they could all get a good look. Any Iron Guardist who could be found in Ploieşti was hunted down, shot and dumped in a prominent location. The purge was pursued in similar fashion all over the country, until hundreds had been put to death. 'Exemplary punishment', 'irrevocable measures': these were the terms under which the king exercised his iron fist – he was Prussian, after all – to 'wipe out the remnants of the Iron Guard'. With the bloated bodies still swinging from lamp posts, an official communiqué stated that 'there is now perfect order in the country'.

Order, of a kind never experienced before, was also coming to Poland. By 8 October 1939 Polish resistance had collapsed, leaving Hitler and Stalin to annex their spoils. Under the terms of the German–Soviet Frontier Treaty, they snapped the country in half like a biscuit. The Soviet portion was incorporated into what is now Belarus and Ukraine, while the German portion was absorbed into the Reich as the *Eingegliederte Ostgebiete*, or Incorporated Eastern Territories, whose soil and people were to be immediately Germanised. Place names were changed, new maps were hurriedly printed. The country known as Poland had ceased to exist.

'Not a word of the disturbing events taking place in Romania and elsewhere was ever discussed by my parents in my presence,' Roy Redgrave later recalled. The adults were hiding things. 'Not in front of the children' was a refrain I heard often in my own childhood, and it always struck me as odd – a way of confirming that something was wrong, while trying to conceal it. But in late 1930s Romania, to hide the truth from children (or the bits of it that could be known) was to reduce the risk of them blurting out some indiscretion. This was now a suspicious and dangerous place, especially for foreigners. The secret police were everywhere, and animated conversations at the workplace or even at home (especially if you had servants) were replaced by coded, muffled exchanges. At the Athénée Palace in Bucharest the word 'espionage' was hissed throughout the hotel. In its rooms and suites, foreign correspondents and the assorted crazies and carpet-baggers who come out of the hollows when war is mooted locked up their papers and searched along the picture rails for the wire of a Dictaphone.

Waiters, barmen, valets, porters, chambermaids, lavatory attendants, the hairdressers and barbers in the beauty parlour, the pageboys in their turquoise uniforms with little monkey caps strapped around their chins – practically every employee at the Athénée was on the payroll of Carol's secret police, or German secret agents, or Italian, American, British or French agents, or all of these. After closely observing the 'apple-cheeked' pageboys, one American reporter residing at the Athénée concluded that they were best placed for the job of surveillance:

> *Theirs was a strategic position. They had only to turn their heads with the little monkey caps to the right and they could watch the revolving door, the entrance hall, and the desk. Turning the monkey caps to the left they could see the lobby, part of the bar, and most of the green salon beyond it. Before their noses were the stairs, the two elevators, and the telephone booths … They told what people ate and for how much and with whom, who came to see them and how long they stayed, what they said. If there was nothing to tell, they made it up.*

Gone were the days when political events could be argued over loudly in cafés and restaurants, or at the cocktail parties hosted by the Redgraves at their house overlooking the River Doftana. Visitors to the house now dwindled to a small cadre, mostly people from the oilfields. I look at their names in the guest book and I want to shout, 'Get out of there. Go. Now!' I am sitting in the crow's nest of history and I can see what's hurtling towards them.

FOUR

Over the radio
I hear the victory bulletins of the scum of the earth.
Curiously
I examine a map of the continent. High up in Lapland
Towards the Arctic Ocean
I can still see a small door.

Bertolt Brecht, 'The Darkest Times'

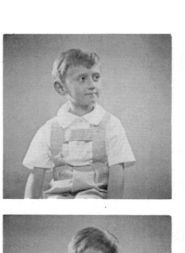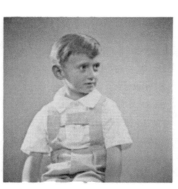

MY FATHER'S HOUSE in Wiltshire backed onto the Kennet and Avon Canal, which used to connect Bath and Reading, but fell into disuse after the opening of the Great Western Railway in 1841. When we walked on the towpath in the 1970s it was neglected and overgrown, the perfect conditions for huge, juicy blackberries. Close to a humpback road bridge that spanned the canal there was a small pillbox, an ugly concrete hexagon with tiny openings in its thick walls. It had a doorway without a door, but immediately you entered there was an L-shaped blast wall, so you had to make a tight right and follow the wall in almost total darkness for four or five nervous paces before arriving in the interior.

The temperature immediately dropped, the walls were green with damp and the floor was scattered with cigarette butts and tiny, shrivelled plastic bags. The embrasures were placed too high for me to see out of and were much narrower inside than outside. Here and there was graffiti: a repeat motif was a heart with an arrow through it, with initials on either end, but there were also forbidden words like 'piss' and 'fuck', which no doubt described the principal activities (hence the stench and the condoms) that were conducted in this dismal, airless space. I hated it and only went inside a couple of times, probably dared on by my brother, Alexander. Daddy always walked straight past it. A bit further on, next to a lock, there was an even smaller pillbox, but I never got beyond putting my foot in the doorway.

When we asked Daddy what these pillboxes were for, he said they had been put there during the war in case the Germans invaded, but this had never happened and they were just left there. How strange, I thought, that anybody had ever taken seriously the possibility of sending an army down the Kennet and Avon Canal. How would they squeeze down this thin ribbon of water with its locks that took for ever to open? On a narrowboat?

There were other bits of the war lying around – an abandoned aerodrome with acres of cracked concrete where Daddy took us to 'drive' his car (Alexander and I taking it in turns to sit on his knee and hold the wheel while Daddy accelerated to a stately crawl); an air-raid siren that was stored in the 'big house' in the village and dragged out onto the lawn for testing once a year – but the war itself, as opposed to its random leftovers, never insisted its way into my childhood imagination. Only now do I wonder what my father might have been thinking when we watched *Dad's Army*, our favourite television series, with its opening sequence of swastika arrows spreading across France towards the English Channel, prodding, probing, before shrinking back to the tune of 'Who do you think you are kidding, Mr Hitler?' Alexander and I thought it was very funny.

In the window of the German propaganda bureau in Bucharest was a large map of Grossdeutschland. It was an interactive map, eye-catching and, in its sorry way, informative. Few people walked past without gazing in the window, in much the same way as they checked out the displays in the Lafayette department store just up the boulevard. It worked like this: whenever Germany made a move on its ancient *Heimat* – Austria, Sudetenland, the rest of Czechoslovakia, Poland – cardboard arrows were placed on the map to signal the implacable advance; and, when the deed had been accomplished, the arrows were replaced with cardboard swastikas. The fate of nations, of millions of lives, described in a few square inches of cutouts moved around on a flat projection. Geography as board game.

In short order it became necessary to introduce other maps, because Grossdeutschland didn't quite capture the scope of Hitler's real ambitions. The British information office, which was directly opposite on the same boulevard, took up the game, with generally poor results. Olivia Manning, loosely disguised as Harriet in her fat chronicle *The Balkan Trilogy*, provides the following commentary on how it proceeded:

> ... she walked ... across the square into the Calea Victoriei and, passing through the parrot-land of the gypsy flower-sellers, reached the British Propaganda Bureau. No one was looking at the pictures of British cruisers that curled and yellowed in the sun, but there was a crowd round the German Bureau opposite. Curiosity propelled her across the road.

> The window was filled with a map of Scandinavia. Arrows, three-inches wide, cut from red cardboard, pointed the direction of the German attack. In the crowd no one spoke. People stood awed by the arrogant swagger of the display.

This was 9 April 1940, and the arrows announced the invasion of Denmark and Norway. During the following week the arrows thrust the Norwegians back and back. The British information office, meanwhile, had replaced the faded holiday-cruise posters with its own map, on which the loss of the German destroyers at Narvik was 'restrainedly marked in blue'.

Every morning the passers-by, lured by these first remote moves in the war, crossed the road to compare window with window; but it was the blatant menace of the giant red arrows that held the crowd.

On 10 April the red arrows on Denmark were replaced by a swastika (the campaign was over in six hours). Over the following weeks the red arrows on Norway and Sweden were also retired, in favour of swastikas. The map was then removed, and the window remained empty.

No one was much impressed. The move had not, after all, been the beginning of events. It seemed a step into a cul-de-sac. The audience waited for more spectacular entertainment.

On 10 May, Harriet and her friend Clarence were driving along the Calea Victoriei when their car was held up by the press of people in front of the German Bureau.

Harriet said: 'There's a new map in the window.' Without speaking, Clarence stopped the car and got out. Rising tall and lean above the heads of the Romanians, he stood for some moments and gazed into the window, then turned in a business-like way and opened the car door. 'Well, it's begun,' he said.

'What do you mean?' Harriet asked.

'Germany has invaded the Lowlands. They've overrun Luxembourg. They're already inside Holland and Belgium. They claim they're advancing rapidly.'

On 11 May, Liège was blotted out by a swastika; Rotterdam followed, then Antwerp. More arrows, to signal the German advance through the Belgian Ardennes. (Not shown on the map: France's Grande Armée falling back before it could put its boots on; roads congested with fleeing soldiers and civilians, who were bombed and machine-gunned for days by the Luftwaffe.) On 15 May arrows showed the direction of the final push towards Paris and the English Channel. By 25 May there was a swastika sitting on Boulogne; less than a week later, on Dunkirk.

By now it should have been clear to everyone who looked in the German window that the arrows could only ever go forward, else what would be the point? In the window opposite, the British were missing a trick: their arrows were going backwards, across the Channel from the beaches of Dunkirk, which had been modelled as a sandbox with little ships standing in a sea of blue wax – a pitiful piece of propaganda, though not as pitiful as the truth.

Every day the crowd around the German Bureau window saw the broad arrows of the German advance stretch farther into France. One crossed the Somme and veered south towards Paris. The spectators said that surely, some time soon, there must be a stop.

On 12 June the arrows indicated that the German Army was twenty miles from Paris. (Not on the map: David and

Wallis Windsor leaving France in a convoy of cars loaded with their luggage.)

> *When [Harriet and Clarence] drove up the Calea Victoriei, they saw that the illuminations had been switched off in the Cişmigiu. The park, where people walked in summer until all hours, was now silent and deserted, a map of darkness in the heart of the subdued city.*
>
> *Clarence said: '"The Paris of the East" mourning her opposite number.'*
>
> *In contrast, the German Bureau window was brilliant with white neon, and still drew its audience. They saw, as they passed, the red arrows, open-jawed like pincers, almost encircling the site of Paris.*

On 14 June, nine months after France and Britain had declared war on Germany, the arrows surrounding Paris were removed and the city was swatted by the swastika. (Not on the map: a German military band playing the 'Hohenfriedberg March' in front of Notre-Dame.)

During the first months of the war the high point of French propaganda had been a huge world map, posted everywhere, portraying the Allied countries with their colonies in glowing red, spread all over five continents, whereas Germany was drawn as a forlorn, tiny black spot in the centre of Europe. The caption read: '*Nous vaincrons parce que nous sommes les plus forts*' – 'We shall win because we are the stronger.' The price for this delusion, this 'Maginot Line of the mind', as the Nazis called it, was total defeat. The French were now tenants in their own country – they couldn't even make maps of it without the consent of their German landlords.

The irony in all this is that the Maginot Line never fell: in a reverse compliment, the Germans had simply skirted around it, attacking through the undefended Ardennes forest. Technically the French were right to claim they had erected the greatest fortification since the Great Wall of China, but their fatal mistake was to believe in their own propaganda, in the myth that power and permanence could be achieved by walling themselves in. All defensive walls (and what wall isn't defensive?) are doomed to fail in the end, as their ruins tell us. To trump it all, sections of the Maginot Line were not even French, but German – fortifications built by the Kaiser before the Great War, only to be surrendered to France in the Versailles Treaty and refitted at exorbitant cost by Monsieur Maginot. Back once more in German possession, these redoubts were put to timely use as stockades for interning French prisoners of war.

Right up to the fall of France, *The Times* could be purchased at a newspaper booth on the Calea Victoriei every day at two in the afternoon – the same edition as appeared in London that morning. Like the Orient Express, which traversed the continent from London to the Golden Horn, the long reach of *The Times* announced the epic destiny of a borderless world. That neither was arriving in Bucharest any more – the 'Magic Carpet' had stopped running at the end of 1939 – was confirmation not only that Romania was cut off from Western Europe, but that Western Europe itself had been taken out of service.

Trapped in the Balkans: this had long been a theme of Orient Express novels, most of them penned by Westerners who associated Eastern Europe with low-hanging fog and assassinations, and were therefore grateful to be luxuriously sealed behind glass and steel in 'a sort of tinned Occident', chewing up the foie gras and not the minatory landscape beyond. There were Easterners, too, who indulged in this uneasy view; Easterners who never thought of themselves as Easterners, such as my grandmother, Elena, whose horizon was filled with the West, with Vienna, Paris, London, all of which were so agreeable, so civilised. These were the places she felt most at home in.

For her children, Donald and Peter, these were the places that postcards came from, bearing news of their parents' travels and previously unseen stamps to be soaked off. These places were not home, because home is the place you come back to, where you unpack your suitcase and give out the presents you have brought with you, and put your clothes back in the drawers and the suitcases back in the cupboard. Most children, unless psychopaths or arsonists, are instinctively conservative: for them, there is no place like home. So how do you begin to explain that home might have to be found somewhere else?

A few years ago I was flicking through one of my father's books when a contact sheet of photographs fell out. They show his child-self posing for a studio camera. He's about eight or nine. He looks straight at the lens, serious, cowed (these images I cut out and threw away), except in the last few shots, where he seems to be responding to someone or something out of frame – his expression changes, there is the trace of a suppressed giggle and then, as if prompted to let it out, he does. A sweet little boy who has escaped from whatever it was that made him look so tense just a few seconds earlier.

There were about twenty shots on the sheet. Two were marked in ink with a small x and were among those I discarded, because Donald looked so uncomfortable and they reminded me of a certain atmosphere (sky falling on head). I now see this must have been a sitting for a passport photo, most likely in late June 1940, when every British subject in Romania was required by the British Legation in Bucharest to get transit visas for all neighbouring countries, against a possible evacuation.

France had just fallen, Hitler bestrode the continent of Europe, from the Arctic Circle to Bordeaux, from the North Sea to the Vistula. Save for the Baltic States, Spain, Switzerland and the Balkans, the Nazis had battered or menaced all Europe's sovereign nations out of existence. Romania's frontiers now faced Soviet Russia and German-occupied Poland in the north and north-east, pro-German Hungary in the north-west and west, Yugoslavia, and traditionally unfriendly Bulgaria to the south. The perfect circle, encircled.*

Within, the country had become airless, struggling with the revenant fascist Iron Guard and the Nazi fifth column that was funding and training it. There was also the problem of tens of thousands of Polish refugees (those who had survived the winter), and innumerable peasant women and children who, having lost their breadwinners to conscription, were now reduced to beggary. They, too, had died in great numbers during the winter. In Bucharest their bodies, often frozen together in bunches, were collected every morning by cart and thrown into a communal grave.

Many of the British community – unpersuaded by Carol's assurance that the Balkans would not disintegrate, that Romania would hold its position – had already left after the Călinescu assassination and the purge that followed. Most of the Americans had also gone, including those thrilling Texan oilmen who would shoot their

---

* To the east lay 270 miles of Black Sea shore.

revolvers at jerrycans, *onetwothreefourfive ... just like that.* It was now illegal for foreigners to own or carry arms. Donald had an air rifle, but no interest in using it, after shooting the songbird off a telegraph wire. There was also a 16-bore shotgun, which Joe hid, just as Robin Redgrave hid his .45 revolver, a shotgun and two sporting rifles (before going back to boarding school, Roy had smothered them in grease, wrapped them in sacking and stashed them in the long, overhanging eaves of the Doftana house, where they might still be). There were other restrictions: foreigners could only move from one locality to another with special police visas; all *permis de séjour* had to be renewed monthly; everybody, including children, was required to report to the police station for identity checks. Fearful for all of them, the British Legation insisted they fill in a form giving religion, next of kin and whom to notify in the event of death.

Despite all this, my grandparents stayed, as did their close friends, the Redgraves. I don't know if the Redgraves spoke German – certainly that was the language spoken in the Słomnicki household, while Robin and his wife, Micheline, conversed in English and French. By the summer of 1940 it was sensible to speak German if you could. There was now a swastika flag falling three storeys down to the porch of the Athénée Palace (it had previously put out a Union Jack), and its English Bar had been symbolically occupied by the Germans – journalists, businessmen and members of the huge embassy retinue, most of whom were spies or Gestapo.

Why not leave, when they had British passports and a homeland in reserve? Why linger, when every exit door was slamming shut? Unlike most of their expatriate colleagues and friends, the Słomnickis and the Redgraves were not merely stationed in Romania, to return at some point to their homes in Surrey or Yorkshire where they might be persuaded to give a talk to the local Rotary Club about their adventures in the edgelands of civilisation; for Elena and Joe, Robin and Micheline, everything they had was here in Romania, and everything is always too much to lose. Or could there be another explanation, something that was never talked about in front of the children, then or later? Either way, they stayed and watched a country die.

Never in the past twenty years had Hungary, Bulgaria and Russia renounced their claims on the provinces lost to them. In Hungary flags on official buildings had been hoisted at half-mast all this time, and families sitting down to a meal would not touch their goulash before loudly declaiming, *Nem! Nem! Soha!* – 'No! No! Never!' None of these nations would act against Romania as long as France, the country's foremost supporter, was still considered Europe's most formidable military power. Now that the Germans had punched France out of the equation, and with Hitler's connivance, they could all pounce.

On 26 June 1940, three days after the French surrender, the Soviet government issued an ultimatum: Romania must give up all Bessarabia ('robbed') and northern Bukovina ('compensation') within two days. All military materiel, railways, rolling stock, bridges, depots, aerodromes, factories, power plants and telegraph installations were to be handed over in good condition. For forty-eight hours the king and his ministers temporised. True to their word, the Soviets landed their planes in both provinces on 28 June. Romania acceded, and begged for more time to organise the evacuation. They were given a few hours, and then Soviet troops were sent over the border.

The king commanded his officers to retreat with their men, chests out and heads held high. This is not what happened. Pell-mell they fled, officers first, followed by bewildered regulars and reservists, some of them so slow off the mark they had already been disarmed by the enemy. Left to their own devices were three and a half million civilians – ethnic Germans, Poles, Jews, Hungarians, Ukrainians, Romanians; the baronial rich with their Aubusson carpets and silver chandeliers; black-gowned, bearded Jews with the keys to their synagogues; peasants with little more than their sheepskin jackets, those 'people who [had] grown out of their soil, with hair like grass, with skin like bark, with hands like tree roots'.

Territorial revisionism, the tragic muddle of the unmixing of people. The border change set in motion a double stream of fugitives: ethnic Romanians, Austro-Hungarian landowners and the wealthier Jews poured out of Bessarabia, while crowds of poorer Romanian Jews headed into it, in the hope of finding in Soviet Russia a refuge from a regime that was fast becoming violently anti-Semitic. The contra-flow of refugees traversing the same roads and bridges was further congested by a change of mind, of people turning around and going back towards their beloved homesteads after an exile of less than forty-eight hours. But where exactly was the border? Attached to the ultimatum was a small map on which the ceded territories were roughly marked by a red line drawn in pencil. The thickness of the line on the map, covering a seven-mile band on the ground, made it impossible for the Soviets to know with certainty the limits of their new possession. It wasn't a question of standing on the line, but in it.

Within a week the Soviet occupation of Bessarabia and Bukovina was complete. Romania had lost 12,000 square miles and been pushed back to the pre-Versailles border, where rusty barbed-wire entanglements from the Great War still straggled through the countryside. In Bucharest the flags were at half-mast and the songs that rose from the Roma violins in the cafés were old laments of oppression and foreign masters.

Next to pounce was Bulgaria, with the demand for a slice of the southern province of Dobruja, historically a disposable counter in Balkan politics. The king and his ministers caved in and, by 21 August, Bulgarian troops were massed at the border, ready to march across as soon as the final agreement was signed. Then it was Hungary's turn (I seem to be rushing this – the death of Greater Romania in a few paragraphs – but if this were a map, it would be to scale). Hungary had been set on its relentless revisionist policy since 1919 and was sticking to it without compromise. On 1 September, Romanians learned that the north-western half of Transylvania was to be ceded to Hungary within forty-eight hours.

In Transylvania peasants gathered on the roads, begging their retreating soldiers, eyes downcast in bitter humiliation, not to abandon them once again to 'Hungarian slavery'. In vain. The Hungarian–Romanian joint border commission was already fixing the line of the new frontier on the ground and replacing signposts to incorporate the former Hungarian place names. The small town of Margitta, for example, was now to be known as Marghita. For its Jewish population, that exchange of a single consonant signalled catastrophe. A young boy, Ladislaus Löb, later told of the moment the Hungarian troops arrived:

They were greeted in the Main Square by veterans of the First World War. These included about a hundred Jews, who were wearing their medals and welcomed the Hungarians with open arms. The leader of the Hungarian troops, a Colonel Szonyi, ordered the Jewish veterans to leave before he allowed the celebrations to

*continue. One of our neighbours was overheard saying
to the Hungarian soldiers: 'Thank God you're here.
We didn't know what to do with these Jews any more.'
On the next day the arrests of so-called communists or
collaborators with the Romanians began. Most of those
arrested were Jews, and most of the charges were false.
Such harassments were to continue until there were no
Jews left in Margitta.*

Romanians showed little concern for the Jews of
Transylvania, who were so obviously extraneous to the law
of blood and soil, with its natural hierarchy of belonging
and rights. All 'true' Romanians held Transylvania to be
the cradle of *their* race; it was there that 'the first light was
kindled, the warm love of our country, the consciousness
of our national unity, the sentiment of freedom and honour
were born'; there that the graves of their martyrs were to
be abandoned to the enemy.

That which is sacredly and eternally Romanian: in less
than two months, Romania had lost nearly half its territory
and population. Her borders, having been shoved inwards,
left most of the Carol Line on the wrong side. If Greater
Romania was an opera set, it had a kind of technical beauty:
Act One had been the performance of the perfect circle;
Act Two, rectification, was simply Act One in reverse.

WHAT TO TAKE?

Hannah Arendt took her mother. They passed through the
front door of a house in Germany and left by the back
door, which was in Czechoslovakia. Freud took his couch.
Einstein took his violin. Brecht passed out of Finland
through 'a small door' high up in Lapland, with his wife,
his mistress, his children and twenty-six suitcases. Alma

Werfel, who escaped France across the Pyrenees to Spain, set out with seventeen pieces of luggage – enough, someone said, for a hundred-strong Sherpa expedition. It was all essential, she insisted, because the suitcases included music scores by her dead husband, Gustav Mahler, and the original manuscript of Bruckner's Third Symphony. There was also cash and her large collection of jewellery, though I doubt she mentioned this to the people-smugglers who guided her over the mountains. She eventually succeeded in bringing it all – and herself, undiminished – to the United States.

Béla Zsolt, fleeing Budapest for Paris a day before the outbreak of war, took nine suitcases: 'all my possessions, my clothes and my wife's clothes and all the necessities and small luxuries we had collected in our lives: the objects, the fetishes'. A bad decision: the obsession with the suitcases took them in the wrong direction. During the course of the war the nine suitcases became a knapsack, the knapsack became a shoebox, and the shoebox became a box of biscuits given to him by an acquaintance. Once he had eaten the biscuits, Zsolt had no more luggage.

Marcel Duchamp took his *Bôite-en-valise*, a box within a suitcase that contained miniature replicas of sixty-nine pieces of his work, including the infamous urinal. Disguised as a cheese merchant, Duchamp made three trips across Nazi checkpoints between Paris and Sanary-sur-Mer, carrying a large suitcase containing the material for his portable museum. Once it was complete ('My whole life's work fits into one suitcase'), he managed to ship it, and himself, to New York.

Royalty does it differently. Arriving in neutral Portugal after the fall of Paris with as much stuff as they could fit into their suite of cars, David and Wallis Windsor immediately turned their attention to getting the rest of their belongings forwarded to them by the occupying Germans, who were happy to oblige. Working from an inventory that was specific, down to the table napkins – who better than the Nazis to handle an inventory? – officers of the Third Reich loaded up the trucks and sent them on their way to Lisbon.

King Carol, soon to join his Windsor cousin in the ranks of the regally unemployed, could not depend on such cooperation from the Third Reich or its stooges in Romania. Chief stooge was Ion Antonescu, a career general who forced the king to abdicate in favour of the eighteen-year-old Michael on the evening of 5 September 1940. The coup granted Carol Hohenzollern the distinction of being the only European sovereign to be succeeded twice by his son. 'King Carol Goes Again', ran the headline in *The Times*, as if reporting Ivor Novello's latest song.

He left on a train before dawn the following day with his Pompadour, Madame Lupescu, their pets and servants, and nine carriages piled high with treasures, including Carol's priceless stamp collection. This was noticed too late, and pursuing cars of Iron Guardists narrowly missed halting the train as it crossed the border into Hungary at Timişoara. They machine-gunned the train, but the driver put on speed and got away (according to one account, Carol had ducked into a bathtub for shelter; another held that he had flung himself on Lupescu to protect her). The train, with drawn blinds, passed through Yugoslavia (whose king, Peter – Carol's nephew – would soon be following him into exile) and arrived at Lugano in Switzerland on 8 September. Eventually Carol and Lupescu made it to Portugal, with all their loot intact.

Under his royal dictatorship, Greater Romania had become a map without a country, for which crime Carol's enemies had gathered round to ensure his downfall. Such prestige as he had left was shredded, and it was no coincidence that he had chosen this moment of national humiliation to invoke that historical scapegoat, the Jew. A month before he fled, he signed a series of anti-Semitic laws, under whose severe restrictions Romania's 800,000 Jews were to be barred from all public office including the army (instead of doing military service, they would be taxed or, if too poor, engaged on public works, a euphemism for slave labour), forbidden to own rural property (Jews contaminated the soil), and no Jewish child was allowed to join the official youth movement set up by Carol in 1935.

It must have pained Carol to see his mistress pursued for years by the lurid, sensational headlines of Goebbels's propaganda outlets, which positioned Lupescu as a chief plotter and representative of 'the international, criminal Jewish clique'. In cleverly retouched photographs, published throughout the German press (which was widely circulated in Romania), she was given swarthy features, narrow eyes, a hooked nose. Captions and copy told of her 'ghetto birth' in the most squalid circumstances; of her climb to eminence in the royal court through cunning, subterfuge and the exercise of unsavoury talents. As applied to Lupescu, the king might well have recoiled from such offensive conceptions of Jewishness. Or maybe he didn't. Maybe, by privately denying her Jewishness (as did she), his conscience was untroubled by the promotion of anti-Semitism in the public sphere. As for the Romanian holocaust that was organised by his political successors, I can find no record of Carol's disapproval.

It's hard to find a credible defence for Carol, although Prince Paul, his grandson by Zizi Lambrino, could be admired for attempting it. Unfortunate, therefore, that he includes a parse of Carol's private diary for the bitter winter of 1939–40, in which we find the king relaxing with his mistress, shooting and fishing, playing poker and back-gammon, reading, watching films and concentrating on his stamp collection, which presumably boasted every set of first issues of himself. This, while peasant conscripts were barely subsisting on the hypothermic Carol Line and their families went without bread, which was taxed to build it. At the time of Carol's departure, the output per acre of a typical Romanian peasant was the lowest in Europe, the total sum of his assets a wooden plough and a solitary pig.

Ultimately the most telling legacy of his reign was an unfinished palace. The unpopularity of his decision to tear down much of the centre of Bucharest to build it should not be underestimated. Carol's divorced wife, Helen of Greece, thought the plans were ghastly and voiced the general opinion that it was a criminal waste of the nation's money. This impression did not improve when, owing to the architect's miscalculations, the sprawling left wing, already completed, had to be pulled down again. So, there it stood, or failed to stand, a dispiriting metaphor for a nation that had overreached itself.

There is a Balkan prayer that asks for God's protection against glory, important visitors and major events. Keep us safe from history: we choose normality, unbroken days of small repeated gestures, like the train that goes round and round in the window of the department store.

Normality took its leave of the Słomnicki household in stages. After the *Anschluss*, the Austrian nannies and maids had been repatriated to the Reich; and after Romania's large chunk of Hungary was repatriated, so too was the Hungarian cook, leaving Elena, who couldn't boil an egg or iron a napkin, in the hands of Romanian servants who had strange habits and got a bit too close – and who was to say they weren't informers for the Iron Guard? Joe was away for days at a time, mostly at the Steaua Romana headquarters in Ploieşti, which was now operating without many of its British and French engineers, following their recent expulsion for attempted sabotage of oil supplies. That left Elena to go alone with the children to the local police station for identity checks, to sit for hours on hard chairs in a corridor while the police pretended to be busy with other matters; to pass on her own the wild-eyed Iron Guardists who had set up checkpoints all over the town, ever eager to beat someone up; to be alone during the sudden blackouts, with the telephone dead, the random shots fired in the night.

Also gone was the children's au pair, Missie Weldon, back to England before the last land route was closed, arriving in time to savour life in the Blitz, whose terrifying effects were met with heroic quantities of tannic tea or Bovril, banana sandwiches without the bananas, Donald Duck gas masks, Vera Lynn singalongs in musty Anderson shelters.

The new normal. Maybe you can get used to anything once it's happened. For Elena and Joe, and those few British nationals who still remained in Romania, the thing that happened was such a long time coming that it was like a non-thing, a negative space darkly there, waiting to be filled.

During the summer of 1939 – when the Redgraves and the Słomnickis, along with much of the rest of Europe, were on their holiday from the truth – British intelligence officers had been quietly inserted into Romania, tasked with sabotaging the country's oil infrastructure. Since Hitler had a positive interest in Romanian oil – six million tons per year would come in handy, should he open a campaign against the Soviet Union – it followed that Britain and, before she fell, France wanted to stop him getting it.

The object was to disrupt or destroy oil wells, pumping stations and refineries, as well as blocking supply routes to Germany by rail or upstream along the Danube – to which end, a plan was drawn up to blow up the cliffs of the Iron Gates, where the Danube narrows and cuts through the Carpathians in a series of turbulent rapids, whirlpools and submerged rocks. As Kim Philby coolly remarked, 'I had seen the Iron Gates and was duly impressed by the nerve of colleagues who spoke of "blowing them up", as if it were a question of destroying the pintle of a lock-gate in the Regent's Canal.' The operation, as Philby predicted, was a miserable failure, and its protagonists were immediately expelled. *'Des dilettantes! Des idiots!'* exclaimed the Romanian regulars at the English Bar of the Athénée Palace, on hearing news of the debacle.

Worse was to come. Shortly after the fall of Paris in June 1940, the Germans intercepted a train of the French General Staff just as it was pulling out of Bordeaux for Spain. On board was a cache of intelligence documents that clearly showed the extent of the Allied sabotage networks in the Ploieşti oil region – proof, Hitler claimed, that London and Paris had intended 'to burn the Balkans'. Fifty British and French engineers and their families were swiftly expelled, among them Pierre Angot, identified in the captured documents as a member of the coordinating 'general staff' of the Deuxième Bureau (the French intelligence service), which was working alongside British intelligence.

Angot was the technical director of Steaua Romana, working closely with its chief geologist, Joe Słomnicki. Joe was under constant surveillance by German intelligence agents, possibly also harassed by the Iron Guard, and yet they let him stay on. There are two explanations that I can think of: one, that the Germans needed his knowledge of untapped oil deposits; two, that Joe was somehow involved in the sabotage conspiracy but had yet to be exposed. Either way or both ways, he was a hot target for the German *Sicherheitsdienst* (Security Service), which was now firmly embedded in Romania.

The whole Ploieşti oil region was fast being militarised by German 'technical advisers', though SS men in uniform were also seen. Astonishingly, given the risks, Robin Redgrave still had a 12mm revolver in his house. When it was discovered by the local police he bribed his way out of trouble, immediately closed up the house in Doftana – taking great care first to hide the visitors' book – and drove with Micheline and their two daughters to a flat near the British Legation in Bucharest. Everybody was taking precautions. John Treacy, the owner of an oil-well supply business, and his wife Esther had moved into a safer bedroom in their house in Ploieşti after an incendiary bomb had been thrown through a window, and each now slept with a loaded service revolver on the bedside table. Percy Clark had taken a room at the Athénée Palace, reasoning – incorrectly – that he was safer in plain sight. The Słomnickis remained in Câmpina, perhaps believing there was some protection in having their extended family around them: Elena's widowed mother had moved into the top floor of their house, and close by were Elena's brother and sister with their spouses and offspring and in-laws, all of them Romanian nationals.

Had Joe and Robin really been at Constanţa for the whole of August 1939, as Roy remembered? Or did they slip back to Ploieşti for secret meetings with agents of the Special Operations Executive, the bang-and-burn shop created by Churchill in July 1940 with a brief to 'set Europe ablaze'? According to one SOE operative, Geoffrey Household, the sabotage plans were worked up in close concert with a hand-picked team of men from the oilfields. 'They were the salt of the earth,' Household recalled, 'keen, daring, ingenious and refusing to be beaten by any technical problem. All the essential work was done by them. We merely coordinated it.'

Looking through the Redgraves' visitors' book, I find the signatures of several of the SOE officers, including Household, and alongside them the signatures of many of the oilmen implicated in the plot: Jock Anderson, John Treacy, Reginald Young, Charles Brasier, Alexander Miller, Percy Clark. All were visiting Doftana at and around the same time, as was Harold Chalmer Bell, the chaplain who ran the Anglican Sunday School in Ploieşti, so perhaps he was in on it, too. The only signature missing is that of Joe Słomnicki.

The first to be taken was Jock Anderson, who disappeared from Ploieşti on Tuesday 24 September. The following night John and Esther Treacy also disappeared, as did Reginald Young, refinery engineer, and Charles Brasier, both of Romano Americana, and Mr E. Bowden, the drilling superintendent of the Unirea company. Their whereabouts were a mystery for forty-eight hours, after which they were delivered to the headquarters of the *Siguranţa* (State Security) in Bucharest, at which belated point the British Consul was informed. His request for immediate access to the prisoners, now formally accused of being part of a spy network, was denied: the 'interrogation' that had begun in some obscure Iron Guard barracks had yet to be 'completed'.

It was a week before the consul was finally given permission to visit the detainees, and then only for a few short minutes. All had been subjected to 'highly irregular procedures' and 'third-degree methods': they could barely stand properly (blow-lamps had been applied to their feet) or use their arms, which had been wrenched from their sockets from the strain of being hung up on a wall with their elbows tied behind them. They had been given nothing to eat or drink and could only speak in whispers. Esther Treacy, who was being held on her own in a three-foot by three-foot cell, had been pistol-whipped and repeatedly punched in the face. Her husband, John, aged fifty-six, had been tortured so badly that he later needed several operations. It was soon evident that the arrests and interrogations had been carried out by the Iron Guard under the supervision of the Gestapo.

In London the Foreign Office decided to compile a list of 'suitable Romanians in this country for possible arrest as a retaliatory measure', but MI5 couldn't produce any names because their card index of Romanians had been destroyed in the Blitz. New Scotland Yard helpfully stepped in with a list of eleven possible candidates, but cautioned that numbers one and eleven were unsuitable as they had fought with the Romanian Army when Romania was 'on our side in the last war'; two others had left the country, and three seemed to be anti-Nazi and pro-British. That left numbers three, five, eight and ten, all of whom 'should be eliminated at once since their names appear unmistakably Jewish'. Probably the only instance in history in which a sentence coupling the words 'eliminate' and 'Jewish' signalled good news. No further action.

Meanwhile Alexander Miller, the administrator of the Astra Romana refinery, had been snatched from the company's sports club at Snagov, near Bucharest. He was taken to his office, then to his flat, and finally to the *Siguranţa*, by which time his face had been repeatedly slashed with a blade. He was then subjected to further torture. When a legation official managed to get access several days later,

Miller looked 'pitifully dejected'. As did Percy Clark, whose kidnappers, three men with revolvers, had broken into his room at the Athénée Palace, where they gave the sixty-year-old a thorough going over and ransacked his room before leading him out of the hotel through the lobby in full view of everyone. He was taken, as the others had been, to a black hole maintained by the Iron Guard, where he was 'starved, punched and beaten, his arms and wrists cruelly twisted and rendered practically useless'.

If my father, now nine, had started the new scholastic year at his school in Câmpina, this was surely the time to take him out. If wives could be kidnapped and pistol-whipped, who was to say the children wouldn't be next? The situation for British nationals was so dangerous that they had formed themselves into groups, members of which were contacting one another every four hours to prevent a long period from elapsing between disappearances and the beginning of consular enquiries. Joe calling Elena; Elena calling Micheline; Micheline calling Robin; Robin calling the designated contact at the legation, and so on, night and day – normal time put off its course, the house in Câmpina returning the metallic echo of the telephone, voices murmuring on the other side of the wall, Donald and Peter left to their own devices amid many unexplained things.

'We now seem to have reached the point where the Romanian Government are likely to arrest a British subject a day,' the legation warned the Foreign Office. The Foreign Office agreed, telegraphing on 4 October, 'It seems possible that M. Galpin, British manager of Steaua Romana, may be the next victim.' Michael Galpin, Joe's boss, was immediately given a minor post in the legation, bringing the protection of diplomatic status. The British authorities could protest all they liked about the outrageous treatment of the arrested oil workers, but, as they well knew, every one of them (with the exception of Percy Clark) was guilty as charged.

John Treacy was the point man for SOE, which is why he was singled out by his torturers, who worked on him non-stop with the object of forcing him to reveal the identity of the men working under him. In October 1939 he had travelled to London to be briefed at the Victoria Hotel on Northumberland Avenue, accepted the mission, signed the Official Secrets Act and entered the alphabetti-spaghetti world of espionage acronyms as D/H.9. He reported to D/H.5, codename 'Caesar' – the oil engineer W. Raymund Young, whose signature appears in the Doftana guest book (his name was also on the captured French documents, which had led to his expulsion in July 1940). It was Treacy who had recruited his fellow oil workers to the conspiracy, Galpin included; he who had personally directed their activities in the marshalling yards and railway stations on the stretch between Ploieşti and Braşov – cutting brake couplings, filling oil boxes with sulphuric acid and putting abrasives into reciprocating parts of the trains.

Treacy later gave details of his torture in a report submitted to SOE. He had been shackled, beaten on the soles of his feet, kicked in the ribs, repeatedly lifted high off the floor to be dropped down 'as a dead weight' onto his back, so that the heaviest of his tormentors could walk on his chest, then dragged up onto a chair and punched in the face while they 'read out the names of every Englishman and American in the Prahova district [wanting] to know if I knew them and who else worked with me'. Not surprisingly, after fourteen hours of this, Treacy cracked: he confessed his role in the sabotage and acknowledged that Charles Brasier 'had doctored some tank wagons' and Reginald Young had 'also done some work', at which point both men were dragged into the interrogation room from their cells and 'severely fist-punched' in front of Treacy.

The British attempt to deny Hitler Romania's black gold was a humiliating failure. By the time German troops were setting up their *Bockwurst*-and-beer stalls in Ploieşti, SOE operatives were desperately getting rid of their unused explosives, most of which were dropped in a lake. With SOE in retreat from Romania, its salt-of-the-earth collaborators were left 'naked' – intelligence jargon for exposed, without backup – and trailing a lit fuse of evidence leading straight to the sabotage plot: documents, photographs, large quantities of pipe-bombs, switches and other materials that the Romanian police had seized from their houses and offices. Awaiting them was a military tribunal, the outcome of which promised a long stay in one of the hellholes of Romania's Gulag.

As for Joe's role in all this, I don't think the full story will ever materialise. Every bit of information I find is evidence of other information that is missing. And even if I were to spend a lifetime sleuthing for the facts, they still wouldn't give me the whole truth. If my grandfather was indeed a saboteur, what would I make of it? Would it make him important, rather than just an ordinary man doing his best to keep his head down and save his future – family, home, life with a pickaxe amid the majestic slopes of the Carpathians?

Slowly, dimly, the contours of a memory start to form. A scrap of newspaper, brown with age, is being carefully unfolded in the palm of someone's hand. Who? Where are we? A room with windows to our backs, an open door ahead, and beyond that a wall with a long diagonal crack in the plaster. My father is here, and my brother Alexander, but this is not our house. Somebody is handing the scrap to my father. They are talking about it – I don't know what it says. Something to do with his father? A bad thing. I am distracted; someone is holding a glass of white wine, but when it's turned upside-down the wine doesn't fall out.

Perhaps this is not a memory at all, but the sediments of a dream. I can't shake it off, spend hours riffling through all the stuff I have accumulated – books, articles, photographs, letters, emails – but there's nothing that connects to this image, now stubbornly present, of a tiny newspaper cutting. I call my uncle Peter.

'Do you think your father might have been involved in sabotaging the oilfields?'

'I don't know. If he was, he certainly wouldn't have told me. What would be the point? I was only six. And when I was older, he didn't talk about the war at all.'

'Do you remember a newspaper cutting that might have mentioned him?'

'No, I don't. Perhaps you'll find it in the suitcase?'

'Would it be all right if I came over this weekend?'

'Of course,' he answers. 'We'd be delighted to see you.'

The suitcase has changed since I first set eyes on it. After lunch at Peter's house, I ask him if we can have a look. In a small scullery next to the kitchen, he uses a long hook to pull down a folding ladder from a hatch. He slides the sections of ladder down and effortlessly climbs the thin treads. I follow. The attic is smaller than I expected, and he explains that there are other attic spaces in the house, but this one is where the suitcase is. I look around and notice a dented silver teapot, a guitar case, cardboard boxes full of the kind of stuff that oozes its stuffing.

There is the unmistakable, settled smell of attic. I can't see the suitcase, even when Peter points to it, because it's completely different from the one I remember. He notices my confusion. 'It's definitely this one,' he says, slightly defensive, as he drags it out of the eaves. I step forward to look. This suitcase is brown, synthetic leather, with two long, ugly prongs that look like rusty surgical instruments leading into the catches. On one side is a triangular sticker with my father's name on it, D. R. Saunders, in his hand, and the address of his house in Wiltshire, which he purchased in the mid-1970s, though this doesn't help me date the suitcase – he could have had it for years before that. Next to the handle there is a tiny remnant of a British Airways sticker.

I am now in full perceptual lurch, like when the station moves and not the train. *This is the wrong suitcase.*

'Is it possible,' I ask Peter, 'that you decanted the contents of the original suitcase into this one?'

'No, I don't remember doing that,' he answers. 'And why would there be another suitcase of Donald's in the house?'

I describe the suitcase I remember: warped wooden struts, chalk-coloured, weather-blotched, probably made of pressed cardboard, round latches, bigger.

'Well, I think we had a sort of small trunk like that, but I haven't seen it for years. But why would I have taken what's in here out of a different suitcase in order to put it into this one? It doesn't make sense.' The slightest intimation of doubt has crept into Peter's voice – my confusion has spread to him – and I let it drop.

How could I have remembered the suitcase so differently? Have I completely invented this visual memory, or transposed another, entirely irrelevant-to-the-matter-in-hand suitcase onto this one? *Are there two suitcases?* Does it even matter? In Günter Grass's memoir, *Peeling the Onion*, a key detail of the bedroom in the hostelry where he assists a bride and groom to consummate their union is remembered by deliberate misremembering: 'On the wall at the head of the marriage bed hung an oil painting, depicting either two beautiful swans, a couple, or a stag belling.' Use your imagination, he's saying, it's just as true as the truth.

Bending down to release the catches, Peter says, 'Shall we open it?' I say no, and take a step back, but he has already lifted the lid. It's as if he has opened a coffin. I see a layer of folders and the edges of a few documents spilling out of them. On the cover of the top folder, the only one that is fully visible, my father has written, in mortuary capitals, TO KEEP. Peter reaches a hand in to lift it out, but I stage a serious inspection of my watch and tell him *I haven't got time now, I'm going out for supper this evening and there are roadworks on the motorway, you know, just after High Wycombe* – or something like that – which is easier than saying I feel like I have fallen up the rabbit hole. I am completely disoriented, because if my memory of the suitcase is wrong, then what's to say everything else I remember isn't wrong, too? Peter looks disappointed and reluctantly closes the suitcase. We reverse down the ladder, he manoeuvres it back up effortlessly with his eighty-seven-year-old arms and shuts the hatch with the hook. 'Shit!' he says, 'I've left the light on.' Down comes the ladder again and up he shimmies on his eighty-seven-year-old legs to turn it off. And there the suitcase sits, as much in the dark as I am.

When I get home, I call my brother Hugo and ask how he remembers the suitcase. 'What suitcase?' he says. My heart sinks.

'The one you gave me in the car park in the pouring rain after the Redgraves' memorial service. We had to heave it into my car.'

'Um, yeah, I vaguely remember doing that, but I don't know what it looked like.'

'Try,' I say testily. (Am I the only one who gives a damn about this suitcase?)

'Uh, shabby, I think.' Pause. 'Old.' Pause. 'Dark colour?' Then, phlegmatic to the point of sanity: 'Is this for the Dead Daddy book?'

I call my mother. 'Oh dear, I only remember it as a suitcase. Rather tattered. It was very heavy, wasn't it?'

'Yes, it was.'

So many false starts: how many have there been? Where will they lead me, if not to a false stop? Once again I'm left with a dismal sense of futility, of straining to put something that was broken together again, without ever knowing what it was that was broken.

On the morning of Saturday 12 October 1940 fifty Messerschmitts and thirteen Heinkel bombers roared in formation over Bucharest. At the Athénée Palace every room on the second and third floors was hurriedly evacuated for some eighty *Wehrmacht* officers, most of them wearing the Iron Cross first-class beneath their red-lacquered collars. This marked the de facto occupation of Romania, a bloodless victory that included the arrival of 20,000 German troops by road, rail and the Danube, bringing with them motorised forces, tanks, anti-aircraft batteries, anti-tank guns and aviation units. The operation was described by both sides as military cooperation: these were German 'instructors', 'specialists', 'technicians', whose mission was the defence of the oilfields and the training and reorganisation of the Romanian Army. For what purpose? To strengthen General Antonescu's position against internal revolts? Or to fight Germany's battles? A year later the answer to that was clearer. Certainly they were here for the duration: within days, the German military mission had established a brothel for its soldiers, the 'guaranteed Aryan whorehouse', as locals called it.

Five minutes' walk from the Athénée Palace, at the British Legation in Strada Jules Michelet, they were feeding their files into an incinerator. By Monday, all hands were on the telephones in an effort to notify the last remaining British subjects of evacuation plans: they were to leave Romanian territory tomorrow evening by a chartered ship departing from Constanţa; anybody driving there should understand that most of the roads were now controlled by 'military elements'; wiser, if possible, to travel in larger groups by train from Bucharest; all other alternative routes out of the country were extremely ill-advised, following reports of arrests at the frontiers; finally, and with regret, the baggage allowance was one suitcase per passenger.

I don't know what Donald took in his suitcase, except for a couple of his stamp albums. Peter tells me he has no memory of these last few hours at home, but given the choice, he would have asked to take his favourite toys: his Halma set – 'a large circular wooden board with holes drilled all over on which I created patterns with multicoloured marbles' – and a clockwork-driven tank with sparks coming out of the end of the gun barrel as it rolled forward ('What a present for a boy on the eve of World War Two!'). I suppose Elena took her jewellery, including the gold bracelet that had been given to her as barter when she fled the German advance in 1916. What else? They must have made lists. Cash (sterling, not *lei*, which was so devalued that in Bucharest it littered the streets). Winter clothes. Underwear. Shoes. Toiletries. Medication. Documents, already carefully assembled for this eventuality – birth certificates, naturalisation certificates, employment details, passports with transit visas for countries that were now impassable or no longer existed.

Joe took his camera, though not with the same expectations of all those journeys he and Elena had freely undertaken in the fifteen years of their marriage – to England, Greece, Holland, Belgium, France, Austria, Switzerland, Turkey and Syria – journeys unhindered by the low politics of nationalism, where citizens of the world could travel with few or no passport checks, throwing their identity out of the train window as if it were a banana skin. Now, with all continental Europe a huge mantrap, an ever-decreasing zone of possibility, the direction of travel was determined by whatever escape hatch was still open.

Unsurprisingly there is no photograph of Joe and Elena and their sons standing with their suitcases on the pavement outside their house. There doesn't need to be: we know the scene from other photographs that document the story, entirely unexceptional for the times (then as now), of forced departure. My grandparents knew from experience what this looked like, and if they had tried to submerge the memory of their previous flights from home, its reality was now rudely present all around them – those refugees from Poland, Joe's first homeland, as they trudged through Câmpina with their ever-lighter suitcases, possessions dwindling as food had to be bought, and who were at this very moment being rounded up and sent back across the border to become smoke from chimneys.

Joe and Elena, Donald and Peter reached the port of Constanţa on the evening of Tuesday, 15 October 1940, each carrying a single suitcase and wearing as many layers of clothes as possible. There were about a hundred other British nationals assembled on the dock, but no sign of their dearest friends, the Redgraves. So it was without them that the Słomnickis, under the cold stare of Romanian police and steel-helmeted German soldiers, followed their fellow passengers up the slimy treads of the gangway.

There was nothing, in this moment of weeping mooring ropes being hauled into the ship, to connect this place to last summer's holiday on the white beaches, the high-backed wicker sun-chairs that left their pattern on your thighs, the umbrellas under which picnic baskets were opened, the Ştirbei villa with its airy rooms and the minaret overlooking Ovid's Island. There was no sign, as the ship picked its way through the newly laid minefield protecting the port, of the brightly lit river boats that had carried tourists along the Danube to Belgrade, Budapest, Vienna – the heart of Europe, but that lay upstream, and this ship was going the wrong way. There was only darkness and fear as it stole out of port and made for open water, in whose depths German submarines were prowling. As soon as the ship reached the swell, it began to roll. Elena was immediately violently sick.

FIVE

road to left – don't take.
another road to left – don't take.
– between the two left roads there
should be a footpath up to the right.
Zig-Zag path.
Keep to left – steep drop on right.

Extract from directions for a walk, written down
on notepaper by my father

'WHERE'S DADDY?' I asked. 'He's gone away for the summer.' There was a van outside our house and men were lifting furniture into it and other things wrapped in blankets. 'Will he be coming with us?' No reply. Which, in its way, was a reply. I was eight; I knew the game.

I have no memory of packing up our home, just that I was standing on the pavement outside, holding a small colourful box whose lid closed with a tiny brass hook, into which I had put IMPORTANT THINGS: a charm in the form of a water mill whose wheel actually turned, a bright-red (illegal) gobstopper, a polished stone egg, I don't know what else. I was reluctant to let the box go – our new house was only a few hundred feet away in the same West London street; turn left and walk across the railway line with its barriers that lifted and swayed like a pleated skirt – but someone in the van persuaded me to hand it up, said it would be perfectly safe, I'd get it back in a minute.

There was a lot of kerfuffle unloading the van and carrying all the stuff down the long, narrow path that led from the street into a garden in the middle of which, like a secret, sat the little coach house, our new home (but what did home mean, if the meaning of 'our' had changed?). In and out went the removal men, pushing and tugging furniture through the tight right-angle of the short, narrow hallway. And then they left, and all this time I had been waiting to see my box emerge from the upheaval, and it wasn't there. Like Daddy, it was gone.

Shortly after the move, my mother agreed to house-sit somewhere near Hampton Court. I think she was fleeing the damp in the coach house, which came from all directions: downwards through the roof, causing the insulation tiles on the ceiling to detach themselves (one landed on the holy grail, my mother's typewriter); horizontally in the walls; up from the ground (the house had no foundations), rising damp against whose relentless creep visitors were advised to wrap themselves in newspaper from the feet up.

The house near Hampton Court was warm and dry, sunlight poured in through the well-proportioned sash windows. I hated it. It was too big, too quiet. It filled my head with an acoustic flatness, like being behind thick plate-glass. (Is this what ghosts feel like?). It had too many rooms with no people in, and there was a huge cat that would follow me heavily into the loo and stare at my feet as they dangled a few inches from the floor.

I'm not sure when the pilfering started – probably it was a few days in. I targeted the kitchen first and acquired a few ginger biscuits that were too hard to bite into. I took them upstairs and placed under them my pillow. The kitchen yielded nothing else of interest, so I moved on to the other rooms in the house, all of which had the same indifferent smell of absence. In the master bedroom I found a jewellery box sitting on a vanity table. It was empty, but gradually, day by day, I found some form of treasure to place in it: small, shiny things retrieved from the backs of drawers or off windowsills and mantelpieces, a blinking hoard, which I would gaze at in the evenings, before putting the box under my bed and going to sleep.

I woke one morning to find my mother and two strangers at my bedside. The strangers, it quickly transpired, owned the house and everything in it, hence their concern to find that a ring had mysteriously disappeared. There was no suggestion that I had any part in this, but perhaps I could help them find it? Throughout this agonising consultation, I could feel the box under my bed glowing, its heat reaching up through the mattress and into my cheeks. They all went downstairs and, thoughtfully, made a lot of noise to cover my footsteps as I returned the box and its contents, including the ring, to their rightful place.

Postponed understanding, the kind that comes with an audible click. I've only just realised that my magpie thieving was by way of substituting the box of treasure I had lost to the removal van (I can still see it moving slowly across the railway line, the border between before and after); that both boxes were a substitute for a larger loss, and a means to contain that loss by reconfiguring the world in miniature. I still collect small objects; my handwriting is small; my home is small; I am small; I prefer small questions that have answers to big questions that don't.

Objects have a rightness to someone who knows them. Not just charms and whatnots, but the chairs and the table and every other thing that makes up the reality of home. 'You can't love an inanimate object,' my father used to say. He was adamant on this point, yet when I look at the photographs he took of our home (the one we all shared until the van turned up), I see his loving gaze falling on the objects within it: a conch shell on a side-table, a painting by John Piper (a wedding gift), awash with sunlight. Home is never a neutral place, it is a very specific context, an animated expression of the presence it contains. Why can't it be loved? Who knows, at the unrevealed level of atoms, it might even reciprocate.

You can't love an inanimate object. I don't know where he got the phrase from. My suspicion is that it connects to events between Monday and Tuesday, 14–15 October 1940, the last twenty-four hours he spent at home in Câmpina. It's possible that Joe or Elena invoked this rule by way of veto when Donald argued passionately for the things he wanted to take with him – hot tears, desperate pleas as he was divested of some of these things, no doubt impractical to carry, but as important to him as life itself. And just as the crying headache set in, his parents' remorse for the pain caused, the promise that *it will all be here when we get back, it won't be long and Grossmama will look after everything for us.* Grossmama had been living on the top floor of the house since her husband died. And then it dawned on him: *Isn't Grossmama coming with us?*

WANDERJAHRE

Until my father boarded the steamer at Constanța, just shy of his tenth birthday, the distances he had travelled were all completed within a day or a fraction of a day – in the car to the holiday cottage in Poiana, up the bumpy tracks to the oil derricks, to Bucharest on the train. The word 'journey' comes from the Old French *journée*, 'a day's length', with its root in the Latin *diurnus*, 'of one day' (for Roman soldiers, a *diurnum* was a day's rations). This was how Donald had experienced the world: it was never more than a day from the garden gate.

The journey that began on 15 October 1940 lasted four years. But in some sense it lasted for the rest of his life. It carried him away from his childhood, away from his father, away from the longitudes and latitudes, the guiding co-ordinates of his existence up to this point. He soon grew out of asking 'How long will it take?', 'Are we nearly there yet?', 'How long will we be staying here?' He learned that everything was temporary, that home was a 'for now' place, the place where your suitcase was; that, to misquote Isaac Deutscher, trees have roots and refugees have legs because they have to keep on fleeing.*

These realisations arrived gradually, over the coming years, but there was one immediate, definitive change for the Słomnicki family as their ship headed into the pitching, slanting, very black Black Sea. They stopped speaking German to each other. Whether by agreement or instinct, they changed, overnight, the language in which they had all lived together. Elena was now Helen – Mummy, not Mami; Papa became Daddy; the boys were still Donald and Peter, of course, but they had far fewer words at their disposal by which to express themselves, though doubtless there was not much to say on that first, grim night. They were now British – British refugees, to be exact – not just because their identity documents said so, but because their survival depended on it. And thus began my father's second life, as a refugee from a country he had never set foot in.

As the ship moored up in Istanbul the following after-noon, officials from the British Consulate were waiting on the quay. The passengers (Helen sheet-white) picked their way slowly down the gangway and were bussed straight to the consulate, where they were offered sandwiches, tea, cigarettes and more forms to fill in. Peter thinks they were then put up for a couple of weeks in the Pera Palace Hotel,

---

* Upon being asked about his European roots, Deutscher answered, 'Trees have roots, Jews have legs.'

established in 1894 by the Wagons-Lits Company as the unofficial terminus for the Orient Express. Then they moved into a flat somewhere nearby. It had a balcony with a bamboo-cane awning that opened by a winch handle. Unable to resist, Donald and Peter let it out, dust falling on their heads, followed by a bird's nest full of eggs that tumbled onto the tiles and broke.

It was a desolate, broken time for all of them, and they longed to get out. The Redgraves, still in Bucharest, were receiving letters from Istanbul full of depressing tales. 'If you ever have to make the same trip as we have had to do,' wrote one friend, 'for heaven's sake keep clear of this town, unless you have an awful lot of money.' Another wrote, 'We all have our troubles and keep on discussing ways and means of getting out of here. We just pray that you too will still be able to get out of Romania.'

The options for this were narrowing. Percy Clark, who had been released into house-arrest but was too weak to travel to Constanța in time for the boat, was smuggled across the Danube by Harold Chalmer Bell, the chaplain who ran the Sunday School in Ploieşti (the children thought he was a magician and, in this instance, he was). They made it to Sofia and then, under the auspices of the British Legation there, to Istanbul, where Clark was admitted to the American hospital.

He was joined there by the other tortured Britons, who had been released, in the utmost secrecy, between 15 and 29 October. This had been achieved principally by brown-envelope diplomacy: large bribes to senior members of the police and judiciary. John Treacy and his wife, Esther, Alexander Miller, Jock Anderson, Mr Bowden, Reginald Young and Charles Brasier were all hidden in the British Legation until their passports and visas were put in order and then, on or shortly after 30 October, they were spirited out of the country. Legation officials believed that if they were intercepted by the Iron Guard on their way to the frontier they might well be murdered, so I assume their extraction was planned with far greater care than the sabotage plot that had so nearly cost their lives. As it was, recovery in the American hospital in Istanbul took months. When asked by his SOE handlers in London to compose a report at the end of January 1941, Jock Anderson had to dictate it, as he had lost the use of his hands.

Only the Redgraves remained in Bucharest, Robin frantically trying to stave off bankruptcy and praying that Micheline's lifelong friendship with Rica Antonescu, wife of the general-dictator, might afford the family some protection. At 11 p.m. on 9 February 1941 the telephone rang in their flat and a voice speaking in French said, 'Micheline, tell Robin he *must* leave the country *now*. He is in very great danger. No, *not* tomorrow, within the hour. Drive to the frontier; he might still escape.' It was Rica, and the conversation ended abruptly. As Roy tells it in *Balkan Blue*, Robin

> *hastily packed two suitcases, collected his important papers, kissed his wife and sleeping daughters goodbye and slipped out of the back door from the block of flats into the empty street. There were a few agonising moments when his motorcar would not start, but soon he was pushing the Buick as fast as it could go south towards Giurgiu which he reached just as dawn was breaking. He abandoned the car, giving the keys to an astonished official who stood between him and the first ferry which was just about to cast off.*

In less than an hour, Robin had crossed the Danube and was in Bulgaria.

That same day, 10 February, Britain severed all diplomatic relations with Romania. Micheline was contacted by the British Legation and told to report with the girls at the Gara de Nord before 9 p.m. on the 13th for a special train that was to take them, together with the last remaining members of the legation, to Constanţa. Micheline, worried for her daughters and the unknown dangers ahead, took a decision that she was to regret bitterly: she left the girls in Bucharest with their grandmother. On the morning of 14 February the *Izmir* cast off from Constanţa without them and steamed towards Istanbul. Robin, meanwhile, made his way south through Bulgaria, which was primed to join the Axis powers, and in a matter of days he and Micheline were reunited.

I never saw Granny Helen smoke, though I do know that during the war she carried a full cigarette case, as a strategy. I remember only in outline the story my father told me of how these cigarettes – the currency of fugitives – appeased an excitable border guard on a train. I don't know what Proustian rotten egg prompted this story from him, but I remember him saying that the train was *very, very long* and he had explored its entire length to discover there was only one other passenger – *imagine that!* – a man sitting alone in the last carriage; that it was the last train through before the borders closed behind them; that his mother had ignored the counsel of friends to leave by boat and that these friends had chosen that way out but, it was later learned, their ship had been torpedoed and sunk. I remember that as my father told me this in the sitting room of his Wiltshire home, sunlight was filtering in through a confusion of leaves, furry and prickly to touch, on his now-dead mother's scented geranium, and there were dust motes dancing in the space between us. Faced with my urgent question – 'Did your friends on the boat die?' – he turned back and closed the border.

Peter has no recollection of the train, of cigarettes and highly strung border guards, only of sitting in the back of a car gazing at endless orange groves, and someone explaining that because of the war there was nobody to pick the oranges, which was why they were rotting on the ground. All I know is that they moved from Istanbul to Ankara, to a house near the British Embassy, and from Ankara they took the overland route to Egypt via Syria, Lebanon and Palestine (the rotting oranges?), a journey that could only have been achieved mostly by train. They were definitely in Cairo by 26 June 1941, because the day and the place are given on Joe's army record. He was granted an emergency commission as second lieutenant to his old regiment, the Royal Engineers, and was soon posted to Palestine.

Joe, now forty-seven, wasn't obliged to sign up, but there were no other obvious means to support the family. It's possible that, at this moment of deep uncertainty, military service offered him, in addition to a salary, a way of defining himself not solely by the terms of loss and disorientation. Perhaps a life of ordered vagrancy was preferable to the disordered, unknowable alternative; and packing up his troubles in the old kit bag was a kind of replacement effect in which the war – the ultimate distraction from distraction – took Joe outside himself. Is it cruel to suggest also that Helen's obsessive anxiety, her 'always fearing the worst', as Peter puts it, was wearying, claustrophobic? Of all the photographs I've seen of Joe, the ones showing him on active service – sitting on a rock eating from a mess can, pushing a jeep out of the sand, riding a camel – suggest a man most at peace with himself.

Poor Helen, alone and adrift in Cairo in the migraine-white glare of summer, trying to avoid the 'garbage, dung, stench and slander' of the place, as George Seferis described it. According to Olivia Manning, also in Cairo having evacuated from Bucharest and then Greece:

> *All the waste-lots of the city gave out a curious odour, a sweetish distillation of urine, ordure and vegetable decay … At midday there was a rush to get home for the siesta. The trams were so packed that an overflow clung about the doors like swarming bees and several men always fell off as the vehicle took corners at speed. Workmen would lie against house walls and sleep with their arms over their eyes. Everyone … went to bed in the afternoons and awoke to a sense of nightmare and a taste like iron in the mouth.*

For the British – indeed, for anybody except normal Cairenes – it was as if the city had been deliberately conceived as a weeping sore: 'cripples, deformities, ophthalmia, goitre, amputations, lice, flies. In the streets you see horses cut in half by careless drivers or obscene dead black men with flies hanging like a curtain over their wounds.' *Obscene*. This from Lawrence Durrell, who had been living in southern Greece with his family until the Germans invaded, and for whom Cairo was not merely physically disgusting, but morally, too ('this corrupt and slow Nile'). Olivia Manning agreed: the squalor was shocking, but not as shocking as the locals' 'contentment with squalor'.

It's such an English attitude, this inability to forgive the rest of the world for not being England. The way to get round that is to expatriate as much as you can of the mother country into another setting. In Cairo, England Abroad was centred in several prominent locations: Shepheard's Hotel, described by one visitor as like living in the British Museum (even the loos were monumental), its men-only bar jammed with staff officers waving fly whisks and swagger sticks and being indiscreet about the order of battle for the next offensive in the desert war; the Anglican All Saints Cathedral, designed by Adrian Gilbert Scott; the British Embassy with its immaculate lawn sloping down to the edge of the Nile; the Turf Club, an all-male establishment lifted straight from Pall Mall, where members played billiards or sank into deep leather armchairs to read volumes of Kipling, *Sphere*, the *Illustrated London News*.

And there was the Gezira Sporting Club, a vast pleasure ground occupying the southern half of Zamalek, an island on the Nile: 150 acres of gardens with lawns as green and fresh as any in the Home Counties, hosed with Nile water every evening by servants in their white *djellabas*; polo fields, an eighteen-hole golf course, a horse-racing track, cricket pitches, squash courts, croquet lawns, tennis courts, two swimming pools, even a pets' cemetery (surely, for the English, the highest expression of the natural rights of blood and soil). In the clubhouse, khakied officers and British pashas in colonial white linen suits wielded whisky-and-soda highballs or gin slings and talked above the clink of ice about bilharzia and dysentery and the new arrival of Huntley & Palmers' biscuits at Davies Bryan's department store.

Under awnings on the Lido terrace, club members and their guests gathered for a buffet lunch: chicken, game pie, boiled and roast beef, ham and, until the war made this impossible, lamb chops from Romania. No fear of catching cholera here, or leprosy, smallpox, the plague – the club was bordered by an invisible cordon sanitaire of hygiene that also served to ward off the locals, those 'Orientals'/ 'Arabs'/'Moslems'/'Wogs' who were the despoilers of 'forever England' and whose rightful place was in the shithouses that lay beyond its perimeters.

The principle of living in a different country from the one you are actually living in was not entirely foreign to Helen. After all, in Romania she had lived mostly in the comfortably upholstered civility of the Austro-Hungarian Empire, with a few added English and French fringes, the combination of which acted as a screen against too much Balkan reality. So maybe, for her, Cairo was another version of Bucharest, its chaotic, unholy froth something that had to be dodged on the way to the clubhouse of civilisation. The problem was, once she and her thick German accent arrived there, much of the inbred Anglo-Saxon singularity she encountered was alien to her.

Children of migrants or refugees often assume the role of liaison officers, connecting their parents to the new world in which they find themselves. They act as translators and interpreters, not just of language, but of signs, gestures, social codes. There is a significant shift, even reversal, of roles, where the child becomes the mentor, taking the hand of the unsure parent. I think this is how my father lost his childhood.

Before leaving for Palestine, Joe took a flat at Regent House, Zamalek, just north of the Gezira Club. This being the most popular residential area for the *Inglizi* (two nearby blocks of flats were known as Elephant and Castle), rents were high and, as their Egyptian owners tended to remove most of the furniture and rugs, the flats were anything but homely: bare tiled floors, shutters closed against the sun – a complete picture of incompletion. Joe and Helen did what they could to push back the emptiness, bought a few cane chairs and some rugs, a coffee table, some old textiles from the souk to pin on the walls.

I can see it now, because there's a photograph of them in that flat. It's a very strange image, full of tension and obviously staged, but to what purpose? It must be winter 1941 because Joe, back in Cairo from a posting to Iraq, is wearing a jersey under his woollen suit. He sits on one of the cane chairs, holding a newspaper across his lap. On the floor, to his right, is his briefcase – an oversight or intentional? On his left sits Helen, wearing a rope of pearls over a dark dress that has been smoothed over her knees, though a sliver of petticoat is visible. On the wall behind her is a child's drawing of a motorcar. Sitting on a rug by the low coffee table are Donald and Peter. They are both in the uniform of the Gezira Preparatory School – white shirt, tie, woollen tank top, grey trousers for Donald, shorts for Peter, thick woollen socks (they've taken their shoes off) – and each is looking, or pretending to look, at a playing card. Helen is gazing down on them; except she's not, the angle of her eyes is wrong, she's staring into nothingness. Joe is the only one who looks to camera; his expression is crooked and I struggle to read it straight. It's as if he's trying simultaneously to answer and ask a question.

I wonder: could this be a proof-of-life photo, evidence, for official use? Or was it simply a photograph to send to the family in Romania – Elena's mother, her brother Henri and sister Marta? If so, it can hardly have been less reassuring.

CONSOLATIONS

The beaded curtain of Groppi's café in Soliman Pasha Square, portal to a world of wonder – great tubs of ice cream, golden boxes of chocolates on trays, waiters in white *djellabas* with a red sash, pushing trolley-loads of cakes and fresh whipped cream into the enclosed garden, cool in the shade of walls trained with creepers. Decades later, my father's eyes would light up when speaking of it: *the best ice cream in the world*. At Groppi's, perhaps, the feeling of living in the wrong place was fleetingly dispelled.

The Pyramids. Camels. Roller-skating at the Rialto rink. Open-air cinemas (Laurel and Hardy, Abbott and Costello, *Tarzan*). Looking sharp in the blazer and cap of the Gezira Preparatory School. The aquarium in Fish Park on the walk to school. Singing 'All Things Bright and Beautiful' at assembly. Climbing banyan trees behind the Gezira Club cricket pavilion and pretending to be Johnny Weissmuller. Whizzing down the water slide into the swimming pool. Discovering 'high tea': Welsh rarebit, trifle.

Stamps. Donald started a new album, 'EGYPT'. On the first page, a collage of stamps of King Farouk, who, like Michael of Romania, was a boy at his accession. The stamps are the first issue of his reign, designed in 1937. Later in the album we find the revised design of 1944, by which time Farouk was twenty-four and wearing a manly moustache on his rather pudgy face. (Olivia Manning called him 'the fat playboy who treated the throne of Egypt as a day-bed', which may be true, but I'd swap the men in her *Levant Trilogy* for Farouk any day: Dubedat, Lush, Dobson, Gracey, the insufferably virtuous Guy Pringle, and boring old Lord Pinkrose, who supplies one of the highlights of the novel by getting himself fatally shot while delivering a lecture.)

The Farouk collage is mounted around a map, carefully drawn by Donald and framed in black ink. In the middle is Egypt, cross-hatched in green. Surrounding it are 'Anglo-Egyptean Sudan' in imperial pink; French Africa, also pink; Libya, Turkey and Arabia, all in desert-yellow. In this way borders were glued down and the world hinged into place. Donald discovered a stamp shop, Moutran's, and bought a new album. Sometimes he sent himself covers of interesting stamps – 'Xmas Seal for use by British troops in Egypt on their letters home' – posted to Master D. Słomnicki, airmail from Cairo to Cairo, by which I can trace his various addresses. I notice that these envelopes have never been opened. One of them seems to have something in it, but I can't safely peel it off the page, so I take out a small kitchen knife and carefully slice it open on the right-hand side. I pull out two index cards and turn them over. They are blank. What my father put in the envelope seventy years ago turns out to be nothing.

For Donald and Peter there were new friends and, with the arrival of the Redgrave girls, old ones. Ioana and Mary Maud had stayed on in Bucharest with their grandmother after first Robin, and then Micheline, had escaped. Finally in early March 1942, after a hair-raising two-week train journey undertaken by the girls on their own, they arrived in Cairo and into Micheline's arms. It had been an agonising wait for Micheline, who was almost destitute and utterly miserable. Robin had joined the Royal Artillery regiment and been posted to Sudan; and Roy, whom she had last seen more than two years before, was still at Sherborne School, studying for his final exams and firewatching on the roof whenever the air-raid sirens sounded. 'I cannot tell you how I long for peace to come and to be together again in a small place, and to feel secure,' Micheline wrote to Robin. 'I dread this insecurity feeling so terribly, this feeling of not being wanted anywhere.'

A proxy normality established itself – a settling into unsettlement. For a time Joe was based at Middle East Command, whose headquarters were a tram ride away from the flat in Zamalek. The children went to school, Helen and Micheline learned how to douse everything with Mobiltox ('Quick, certain death to all insects'), where to buy groceries and printed cottons for the Greek or Levantine dressmakers to run up some summer clothes. Sometimes, at dusk, they would all walk the few streets to the banks of the Nile, where the scent of jasmine rose in the cooler air.

OUT OF EGYPT

For the past two years the front lines of the war in the desert of North Africa had advanced and receded like the sands on which they were drawn. (If war is a teacher of geography, the desert is the unruly pupil who disrupts the class – deserts blow themselves off the map, which is why putting borders in them is always a silly enterprise.) Back and forth it went, everybody in a state of gritty confusion. Then, in late May 1942, the Axis forces led by Erwin Rommel smashed into the British line from the rear, and a month later his *Panzerarmee Afrika* was streaming across the Libyan border into Egypt. The advance was so swift that units from both armies found themselves going at full tilt in the same direction, trying to avoid each other. As the entire routed Eighth Army poured into Cairo, chaos reigned. German radio broadcast a message to the women of Egypt: 'Get out your party frocks, we're on our way!'; shopkeepers made sure to have photographs of Hitler and Rommel ready to slip into a frame. A curfew was imposed from eight in the evening to seven in the morning.

There was everything to fear – aerial bombardment, street-fighting, an Egyptian uprising – but the British downplayed the panic by calling it 'the Flap', as if it were no more than a dowager's wig being blown off. It was not encouraging, therefore, to see thick smoke rising from the British Embassy and GHQ, where they had started to burn their files. Charred flakes of classified documents fluttered to the ground; such was the heat that some papers were blown intact high in the air, to be recycled into little cones by the (unflappable) local peanut-vendors. There was a run on the banks – the queue of officers outside the military branch of Barclays Bank was half a mile long – and sterling fell so far that it couldn't be given away on the black market.

The queue outside the Thomas Cook office curled around several blocks – women, mostly, desperately trying to secure passage in one of the very few ships leaving from Port Said. Micheline was successful: she got three berths for herself and the girls on the troopship *Queen Elizabeth*. Robin, who was in Tehran, wrote in his diary on 2 July: 'Rommel only 70 miles from Alexandria. What will my poor Micheline do?' The answer was forthcoming. 'Letter today from my dear one announcing her departure for South Africa,' he wrote on 14 July. 'When, oh when, shall

I ever see them again? How miserable I feel.' A quarter of a century after Rommel had broken through the Carpathians, Micheline was once again on the run from his advance.

On 18 July she left with Ioana and Mary Maud from Cairo's central station. It was a madhouse, and the platforms were crammed with every sort of refugee, desperate to attach themselves to any part of a train, including the roof. Many of them were Jews who had already felt the choking geographical dilemma of a world remapped by Hitler; they had fled before, and knew that the survivors were the ones who got away first. The war correspondent Alan Moorehead, who went to the station to evacuate his wife and small daughter, saw a Czech Jew who had been barred from a train try to commit suicide on the platform. Amid the uproar, Olivia Manning noticed that the Egyptian porters were 'slinging the luggage aboard with roars of laughter and shouts of "Germans coming, eh? You go. Germans come".'

Micheline and the girls reached Port Said at sunset, in time to see the *Queen Elizabeth* being coaled, one line of begrimed locals carrying baskets on their backs up a gangway, another line coming down a different gangway with the empty baskets. The ship departed with no escort, headed down the Suez Canal and out into the Indian Ocean, zigzagging and relying on speed to evade enemy submarines. Two weeks later they were offloaded at Durban and found accommodation at a hotel in Kloof, where the girls went to school and Micheline got a job in the canteen of a military airfield.

It would have been entirely out of character for Helen not to panic, so there must be a reason why she and the boys were not on the ship with the Redgraves. Perhaps she simply failed to get a booking. More likely, Joe dissuaded her from going, argued that Rommel would not reach Cairo and that if they went to South Africa they would have a hell of a job getting back. As it happened, just as the *Queen Elizabeth* was carrying the Redgraves away, Rommel's offensive stalled at a railway halt called El-Alamein. Having advanced so fast, he had outrun his supplies, and both sides were digging in after an exhausting month of offensive and counter-offensive. 'The Flap' was over.

Joe stayed in Cairo until he was posted to Iran on 15 September. According to Peter, he worked on plans to sabotage Middle Eastern oil wells in the event that Rommel should carve a German corridor through Egypt. Donald and Peter went back to school, while Helen fretted on her own. In mid-October an extraordinary event occurred in Cairo: heavy, prolonged rain turned the surrounding desert into a garden paradise, as seeds that had lain dormant in the sand for years sprang up and blossomed. And soon after that the second battle of El-Alamein erupted.

Helen, in no mood to stick it out now that Joe was gone, joined the throng outside Thomas Cook, managing to book a passage to South Africa on the *Nieuw Amsterdam*, one of the unescorted 'Monsters' that could outrun German U-boats. The boys were taken out of school, suitcases were packed – again, the torment of what to take – and they sailed out of Port Said on 31 October. On the same day Joe sent a telegram to the flat in Zamalek, telling Helen that he had arranged for them to join him in Tehran. Too late, for the *Nieuw Amsterdam* was already making its way down the Suez Canal. Three days into the journey, as the ship pitched on the high seas and Helen vomited up her soul, the Desert Fox was forced to retreat, tail down and under cover of night, from El-Alamein. By the time the *Nieuw Amsterdam* docked at Durban, the Eighth Army had recaptured Tobruk and the bells of All Saints Cathedral in Cairo were being rung to celebrate the victory. They needn't have left.

As an adult, my father returned to Istanbul and Cairo to search out his favourite sites – the Blue Mosque, the Pera Palace, the Giza pyramids, Groppi's – but he never went back to South Africa and he never talked about it.

This is everything that Peter remembers:

From Durban we travelled by bus right across South Africa to Cape Town. We spent a couple of days there, then we took a bus uphill and downhill for what seemed an eternity. I kept asking my mother, 'Are we nearly there?', and her answering, 'Yes, it will be over the next hill', but it wasn't. Finally, we arrived at Plettenberg Bay, on the Indian Ocean, where we stayed at the Beacon Island Hotel. There was a main building but we stayed in an outlying rondavel built into the rocks with the sea surging between them. There was a sign that said 'NO SWIMMING ALLOWED'. I was cross about this, I couldn't understand why, and then I saw a tiger shark being caught: it was very small but it put up a huge fight, and after this I had no intention of entering the water. I think we stayed here for a couple of months? Then we went inland to a town called George and became boarders at Merchiston prep school. We both hated it. My only recollection is that when my mother came to visit, I cried buckets because I wanted to be with her. That, and the Arum lilies growing wild in the woods at a place nearby called Knysna.

After a term, or maybe two, we went back east, all the way to Pietermaritzburg, where we lived in a

house with another English family, the Mattheys, who
had black servants. Their son, Errol, who was my age,
became my new best friend. I'm not sure, but I think
Micheline and the girls were also there. There were
chickens outside and one day I saw one that had just
had its head chopped off running underneath the
house, which was raised above ground. I remember
Donald in tears after Errol and I told him he couldn't
come into our den, and my mother intervening and
saying, 'You must let him join in your games.'

I shrink from this image of Donald crying, not only
because it conjures the difficulty, in any place, in any time,
of being a child, of the sheer effort required to hold it together
on the sudden, stomach-heaving swerves of emotions, but
also because I know that his childhood sense of being separate and apart came to define him as an adult. True, this
solitariness offered him, on occasion, an enviable freedom,
but mostly it showed itself as an unmovable sadness.

After a desultory year, Helen somehow managed to get
back to Cairo with the children, an almost impossible feat
given the shortage of berths for civilians (for somebody
whose life had long been centred on soirées and tennis
parties – never stooping to pick up the ball – she was
certainly growing more resourceful). Joe having relinquished the Regent House flat the previous year, they found
themselves unpacking their suitcases in yet another new
address, Flat 24, Sharia Kamel Mohamad. Was Joe there to
greet them? His army record from late 1943 onwards shows
postings to Iran, Syria and Palestine, but no doubt he rushed
back to Cairo as soon as he was given leave.

Helen got a job at the British Ministry of Information
as a speaker for the Romanian news service. Every day she

took the tram to General Headquarters, a vast compound surrounded by checkpoints, barbed wire and street hawkers shouting, 'Chocolates! Cigarettes! OBEs!' In June 1944 Micheline Redgrave joined her there, having finally extricated herself and the girls from South Africa. Their names were not given in the broadcasts, but they later learned that their families in Romania had recognised their voices.

Peter, now nine, went back to Gezira Preparatory School where, according to Edward Said, a fellow pupil, the day began in the big hall with the singing of hymns 'accompanied at the piano by the omnicompetent Mrs Wilson and directed by Mrs Bullen, whose daily homilies were simultaneously condescending and cloying, her bad British teeth and ungenerous lips shaping the words with unmistakable distaste for the mongrel-like collection of children who stood before her'. Lessons were 'mystifyingly English: we read about meadows, castles, and Kings John, Alfred, and Canute with the reverence that our teachers kept reminding us they deserved'. Said was much puzzled by the image of Edward the Confessor, 'an elderly bearded gentleman in a white gown lying flat on his back, perhaps as a consequence of having confessed to something he shouldn't have done'. Equally baffling was the tradition of celebrating the king's birthday with maypole dancing in the playground.

Donald was twelve, too old for prep school, so he was sent as a boarder to the English School in the suburb of Heliopolis, where, says Peter, he was miserable. Why this insistence on boarding school? I don't think it was for lack of alternatives; rather that this had always been the plan. Like the Redgraves, who had sent Roy to Sherborne School, Joe and Helen held to the belief that being British was the passport to the world, and that the only way to install an authentic British identity was in the classrooms and playing fields of English private schools. As the young 'mongrel' Edward Said was coming to realise, it was one thing to learn the words of 'All Things Bright and Beautiful', another to appreciate that 'this meant bright and beautiful England, the distant lodestar of good for all of us.'

The muslin strips glued to the windows of the English School, the huge understrutting joists supporting the dormitories above in the event of an air-raid, were reminders of the dangers Cairo had faced, but the city was a much calmer place since Rommel had scurried out of Egypt. By the end of 1943 he was cooling his heels as inspector-general of the Atlantic Wall, a concrete-and-steel monotony that stretched from the northern tip of Norway to the Pyrenees. Erected to express power and permanence, it was – like all such walls before and since – a confession of weakness, a last resort when all other options had failed. Rommel thought it a giant, expensive farce straight out of *Wolkenkuckucksheim*, 'cloud-cuckoo-land'.

Hitler's Thousand-Year Reich was now everywhere on the defensive – not that you would know it from Donald's stamp albums, to which he assiduously applied himself during 'free time' at school. The German issue of 21 March 1943, for example: fifteen scenes of heroic Aryan aggression, including a submarine with a burning enemy ship sinking in the background, Stuka dive-bombers unloading shells, SS soldiers hurling stick-grenades, a Tiger tank smashing through the lines, its turret gun retracting mid-fire. One year on, the mood was more subdued. In the series issued in March 1944 the drama of action was replaced with vigilance: instead of the killer U-boat, a submariner scanning the horizon through his periscope; instead of blazing anti-aircraft guns, a searchlight battery, beside which an officer scans the skies with binoculars; in place of Stukas, a lone reconnaissance plane. True, two of the stamps illustrated the deadly reach of German firepower in the form of a long-range railway supergun and the launch of a flock of V-1 flying bombs (V for *Vergeltung*: vengeance for the Allied bombardment of German cities), but the overall theme was of watching and waiting.

Two months after these stamps were published, the Allies breached the Atlantic Wall on a stretch of the Normandy coastline. Fourteen hours later, it fell. It was the beginning of the end of Hitler's stolen dominion, and to warn the German people of the fact a new stamp was printed. Though it was never as widely circulated as had been hoped, the stamp was published in Switzerland by America's dirty-tricks department, with the aim of fooling the German postal service into inadvertently delivering a portent of disaster right into the homes of German citizens. It was a copy of the definitive twelve-*pfennig* stamp with Hitler's portrait, but with modifications: the Führer's face was overlaid with skeletal features, his jaw half-eaten away, and the subscript was altered from DEUTSCHES REICH, German Empire, to FUTSCHES REICH, Lost Empire.

In wartime you don't get to choose how and when you move around. You take what's offered – if anything is offered at all. It was winter, always winter, when Helen walked the gangway. Once again she and the boys were leaving, but this time they were heading for their own country, on whose soil Donald and Peter had never stood, and Helen only once. In mid-November 1944 they embarked on the *Queen of Bermuda* at Port Said. Before the war, the ship had been a luxury cruise liner in the West Indies, one of the sleek ocean greyhounds that offered a parallel dream to that of the Orient Express. It had a ballroom, a cinema and a swimming pool, and was affectionately known as the 'millionaires' ship'. Now every conceivable inch of it, including the swimming pool, had been repurposed to accommodate troops and stores. Servicemen were quartered in a maze of crowded mess decks, the overspill sleeping on tables and in passageways. Washing and showering facilities were improvised: there was no fresh water available, and the single towel supplied to each passenger was impossible to dry in the damp conditions. Helen and the children were assigned one of the few shared cabins on an upper deck, and spent much of the next two weeks inside it. The weather in the Mediterranean was what sailors call 'dirty'; for the entire voyage the *Queen of Bermuda* rolled and wallowed like a cow in labour.

They arrived at Liverpool docks on 30 November 1944, registered on the incoming passenger list as: Słomnicki, Helen, housewife, 43; Słomnicki, Donald, 13; Słomnicki, Peter, 10. They joined the lines for customs and immigration, were processed and verified as British subjects and then, with their passports and British refugee certificates (twelve shillings and sixpence) stamped, they emerged into a post-Blitz city that was carrying on its business as best it could amid miles of devastation and rubble.

England: bomb damage, rations, cold, rain, skies the colour of depression. Not so bright, not so beautiful.

SIX

Do you feel you belong, do you feel at home? I don't know, I feel most uncertain. My father's house it is, but each object stands cold beside the next, as though preoccupied with its own affairs, which I have partly forgotten.

Franz Kafka, 'Home-Coming'

Moomintroll was silent.

Then he said: 'Somebody's carrying off things from Daddy's house.'

'That's nice, isn't it,' replied Too-ticky cheerfully. 'You've got too many things about you. As well as things you remember, and things you're dreaming about.'

Tove Jansson, *Moominland Midwinter*

I WOKE THIS morning to find I had written a message to myself during the night. I keep a notebook by my bed, mainly to scribble down the trivia that surfaces just as I'm going to sleep, but this wobbly entry must have been caught on the wing of a dream. It reads: *there is no point there is no still point*. My immediate assumption was that what I had meant to write was, 'There is no point. There is still no point', because, grammar aside, that could be taken as an accurate reading of the weather in my head at the moment, a system of low pressure that won't be dispelled. *What is the point of telling this story? Have I reached the point at which there is no point?*

I've always been sceptical about panning dreams for enlightenment. Anthony Burgess, in his now-forgotten book *On Going to Bed*, tells of a man he knew who woke up in the night with the realisation that he had discovered the key to the universe. 'He scrawled on a pad kept on his bedside table the mystical unlocking words. Waking he read them: "All a matter of demisemiquavers. Make much of this."' I can add to that a dream I noted down a few weeks ago, in which I passed a skip painted with the words

'Moot and Skoot Movers'. Waking just briefly enough to register the urgent significance of Moot and Skoot, I told myself it was so important, so obvious, that I must not forget it. What followed was an endless night of waking up, repeating *Moot and Skoot* out loud, then falling asleep again until the night-guard of my conscious self woke me up for another interrogation: *Do you remember? Yes, it's Moot and Skoot.* Eventually, in the early hours, I scribbled it down.

How can something that feels so right, so true in one dimension, amount to such nonsense in the other dimension? Whatever dreams offer us, they don't travel well; they surrender too much at the border post of consciousness. And yet the more I think about last night's dream, the more I see it as a smuggled message: *there is no point there is no still point.* I have immersed myself in a story where departures lead to arrivals that are only ever the beginning of another departure; everything is transitional, there is no still point, because everything that matters – home, belonging, security – is always further away.

And yes, all those suitcases – maybe Moot and Skoot Movers have something to do with that, too. Is the best place for my father's suitcase in the skip? Would that, finally, be the still point?

They say that Jews are never in one place long enough to have a geography, but I know this isn't true because in my father's house there was a framed map of Poland on which somebody had circled the town of Słomniki in red ink. What the map didn't explain was that most of the Słomnickis who had once lived and worked and argued and loved in this town were deported, along with a thousand other Jews of the area, to the Belzec extermination camp between 4 and 8 June 1942; nor did it show the location of the mass grave of the sick and old who, along with infants, were executed in Słomniki before the *Aktion* of 6–7 September, or the pits in the Chodów forest where the corpses of a further 200 Jews were thrown two months later.

The map was also silent about the disappearance of the many Słomnickis who had once lived and worked and argued and loved in other parts of Poland – Łódź, Kraków, Sarny, Olkusz, Bedzin, Warsaw. Nor did it reveal the geography of hell that was superimposed on Poland by the Nazis: concentration camps, labour camps, death-camps, ghettos, all of which had their own internal geographies.

Example: THE GHETTO OF LITZMANNSTADT (the name given to Łódź by the Nazis), which was run as a minuscule kingdom by the vain, dictatorial Jewish elder Chaim Rumkowski. He wore a regal cloak, printed stamps and minted metal-alloy coins with his portrait, and surveyed his domain – all two and a half square miles of fenced-in destitution – from a carriage drawn by a skeletal nag. When the Nazis dumped 5,000 Roma and Sinti in the ghetto, Rumkowski protested, 'We cannot live together with them. Gypsies are the sort of people who can do anything. First they rob and then they set fire and soon everything is in flames.' His solution was to put them in the *Zigeunerlager*, a ghetto within the ghetto.

Example: SOBIBOR, with its neat little cottages with names like *Schwalbennest*, 'Swallow's Nest', or *Gottes Heimat*, 'God's Home', its gravel paths lined with flowers, its vegetable garden and chicken coops – amenities designed for the SS men running the camp, but also to hide its purpose from arrivals, those biological or political category errors who were soon to be herded, naked, down a one-way lane known as *Himmelfahrtstrasse*, 'Road to Heaven', which ended in the gas chambers.

Example: TREBLINKA, with its fake railway station, designed by the camp commandant, Kurt Franz, to trick arrivals there into thinking they were on their way to somewhere else (the one thing the Nazis couldn't stomach was mass hysteria). It had signs reading RESTAURANT, TICKET OFFICE, TELEGRAPH, TELEPHONE, WAITING ROOM, a departure and arrivals board giving train schedules to and from Grodno, Suwalki, Vienna, Berlin, and, above the false door marked STATION MASTER, a trompe-l'oeil clock, its painted hands set to six o'clock. Behind this façade was the extermination camp, its gas chambers signed as shower rooms.

Example: AUSCHWITZ, 'ultimate drainage point of the German universe' (Primo Levi), where the belongings collected at the selection ramp were taken in trucks to be sorted in the warehouses of Kanada – the land of plenty – and, when more space was needed, Kanada II. Two Kanadas, still not enough to contain the landslip of plundered possessions: suitcases (of course), shoes, crutches (nowhere to walk to now), prosthetics, clothes, shaving brushes, dentures, spectacles, wedding rings, bracelets, fountain pens, watches, children's dolls – all scrupulously sorted before being shipped back to Germany, and still surfacing in flea markets and antique shops in Eastern Europe today.

Also in the Kanada warehouses, fumigated lice-free human hair, shaved off the prisoners, weighed and packaged ready to be shipped off in huge bales to be pressed into insulation for detonators, or felt to line the boots of German soldiers, or spun into yarn for use in warm socks for U-boat crewmen. Human beings decommissioned and recycled as raw material for useful things. It didn't stop there: the disassembly line operated even after death. Beyond the gas chambers, the victims' bodies were opened up – unpacked like suitcases – on the dissecting tables in the crematoria in case they contained something valuable. Pliers were used to extract gold teeth, to be melted down and sold on. According to one Nazi boast, this more or less covered the costs of the killings.

Is this where Joe's sisters, Madzja and Henja, ended up, in the human ash-cloud? Madzja and Henja, my father's aunts, about whom I have found virtually no information. Possibly they were living in Warsaw and were trapped there when the city fell to the Nazis on 28 September 1939. Maybe they were lured from there into 'resettlement' by the promise of a loaf of bread and a jar of jam, showing up at a mustering point only to find themselves on a cattle truck heading for the death-camps. Maybe they died from typhus or starvation in the Warsaw Ghetto, or were taken to one of the many secret execution sites – the forests at Kabaty, Chojnów and Sękocin; Wydmy Łuże, Szwedzkie Góry, Łask, Wólka Węglowa – to be shot or gassed in a specially adapted truck and then chucked into a pit.

Census records, telephone directories, ghetto index cards, Yad Vashem, the Wiener Library in London, the International Tracing Service: I've searched not only for confirmation of Madzja and Henja's deaths, but testimony to the fact that they had once lived. I have found many Słomnickis, charted their births and marriages and deaths (mostly in the Shoah), but for Madzja and Henja the records are silent. On Yad Vashem's database there are four and a half million names of victims of the Shoah, which means that one and a half million names are still missing. They are the undocumented disappeared.

I don't know what to make of this. Surely it's impossible to just lose one and a half million people? How on earth can we honour the un-dead dead? Or is it that their very lostness gives them a particular, vital reality: the vanished life as proof of the full magnitude of what happened?

In August 1943, shortly before Helen and the boys returned from South Africa, Joe had been posted to the Middle East Relief and Refugee Administration with the rank of major, tasked with the organisation of some 40,000 Polish refugees quarantined in four tented camps in and around Tehran.

After the Nazi invasion of Poland in 1939, many Poles had escaped south into Romania, where they were initially welcomed. If Joe's siblings had managed to get out by this route, they would surely have found their way to him, so we must suppose they were not among the human stream that, for weeks, passed through or near to Câmpina. In very small numbers, these refugees proceeded through Bulgaria and Turkey, or Yugoslavia, Italy, Greece – wherever they found a gap – and from these countries travelled overland or across the Mediterranean to Syria, Palestine and Egypt.* A far larger number of Poles – more than 100,000, of whom about 6,000 were Jews – came across the Caspian Sea in Soviet ships to Iran. These were a fraction of the 1.25 million Poles who had been deported as 'anti-Soviet elements' to Siberia and Kazakhstan after the annexation of the eastern half of Poland. Two years on, with Hitler now campaigning against his former ally, those who had somehow survived the death-zone were released and evacuated, in a deal struck by Stalin and the Allies.

Of the greatly depleted number who were now under Joe's care in the Tehran camps, there were also some from the western half of Poland, who had run from the Nazis into the authority of the Soviets, only to be loaded onto

---

* Today's refugees use all the same passageways, but in the opposite direction.

cattle cars and dumped in forced-labour camps in Siberia. Was it remotely possible that anyone from Joe's near family might have ended up in Tehran?

A quarter of a century had passed since he had last seen his family gathered in one place. This was in Wiesbaden, before they were scattered by the Great War. After that war, in late December 1919, according to the Special Branch report in Joe's naturalisation file, he had travelled from London to Wiesbaden to be reunited with them. They were all there except for Joe's mother, Zofia, who had died alone in Copenhagen in December 1918. Joe then returned to London to continue his studies at the London School of Mines and never saw his family together again. From various frustratingly low-yield sources, I gather that his father, Bernard, who was living in Wiesbaden with his eldest daughter, Rosalia, died penniless in 1922, shortly after his oil properties in Cheleken were expropriated by the Soviets (Joe applied unsuccessfully to get them back in 1923, and the company was liquidated in the London courts – an early lesson in financial loss). Rosalia died in 1930, aged just fifty-one, leaving two sons by her estranged husband, Felix Gradstein, who had gone back to Poland and died on the Eastern Front from shrapnel injuries in 1944. Their sons both emigrated in their twenties to the United States, probably soon after Hitler came to power. Edward (Teddy), Joe's older brother, went back to Poland in 1920 and married the very glamorous Vala – I don't know her surname, but my mother says she was the daughter of the principal librarian of St Petersburg. They had no children.

Teddy seems to have inherited the Moszkowski musical gene: an accomplished amateur cellist, he once performed in Danzig with the dazzlingly talented pianist Maria Donska. He and Joe got on very well, despite their different outlooks – culturally and emotionally Teddy faced east, while Joe preferred the view to the west. There are photographs of Teddy and Vala visiting Joe and Elena in Romania, including a holiday in Constanţa, and another photograph suggests that Joe once stayed with them in Warsaw. I assume it was Teddy who had arranged for their mother's remains to be transferred from her grave in Copenhagen for re-burial in Warsaw's Okopowa Jewish cemetery, where her sister, Rozalia Moszkowska (mother of the many geniuses, musical and otherwise) was also buried. Perhaps this explains the purpose of Joe's visit. Perhaps he had also wanted to see his sisters, Madzja and Henja.

When I asked Peter what he knew of his aunts, all he could say was that he never met them, and he never heard Joe or anyone else speak of them. But he thought there was a photograph somewhere and, after digging over various clods of papers in his study, he unearthed it and scanned it into an email. It's a studio portrait of the Słomnicki family – Bernard, Zofia, their five children and two grandchildren – taken, at an educated guess, in Wiesbaden in about 1913, a few years after they had left Poland. They're all in their finery and looking comfortably well-to-do. Bernard and Zofia are seated and, between them, on a stool concealed by the rich folds of her velvet skirt, is the eldest child, Rosalia, with her two boys, who look about five and four. Standing behind them are Joe (he must be twenty, and on holiday from university in London), then Teddy, and next to him Madzja and Henja, though I don't know which is which. With the exception of Teddy and Joe, whose body language and expressions suggest independence – Joe especially – the whole family is touching, linked by fond hands that create an easy flow from one to the other.

This photograph, and the passing mention of Madzja and Henja in Joe's naturalisation file, is the only documentary evidence I have that they ever existed. It's not that we haven't tried hard enough to find them – it's that we haven't tried at all. Or perhaps Joe and Teddy did try to find out what had happened to them, without success. A sickening thought: did the Nazis know more about these two women than we, their not-so-distant family, will ever know?

To complicate matters, a letter has just arrived from my mother:

Your father had two uncles on his mother's side, Uncle Ernst and Uncle Norbert. Their father was German, and they lived very well in Romania until Hitler ordered their repatriation at the beginning of the war. Ernst was a <u>convinced Nazi</u> [underlined three times] who prospered in the war and lived happily ever after in a small castle. Norbert was <u>not</u> [underlined three times] a Nazi, and he ended up living with his wife and two children behind dung heaps in a dank farmyard near Ulm, where he repaired motorbikes for a living. I visited them there by train in the early 1970s.

What does this mean? That in my family there were not only victims but perpetrators, or, at the very least, colluders? Where does that leave us: we who remain? Do we get to choose which side we identify with, or does it have to be both? What about neither: is that an option? Muddling the situation even further is a letter from Joe's nephew, Marcel Gradstein, Rosalia's son. His letter, written in October 1978, was in answer to a letter from my cousin Joss, who had traced him to Sarasota, Florida. Joss's letter is lost, but in it he must have suggested that we, Joe's grandchildren, were partly Jewish, which drew this answer from Marcel:

Now to your theory. I am afraid I totally disagree with you, as the facts do not bear it out. Let me emphasise, I consider myself 100 per cent Jewish, and am proud of that ... As to your grandfather Joseph and his brother Edward, they were converted Jews ... I do not know, but it is hard to qualify it as an act of

heroism. Whether you are Jewish, is a matter of defi-
nition. You be the judge.

I don't know to what extent Joe considered himself to be Jewish, only that Hitler would have happily had him and his children on a transportation list. I'm not sure how he could have converted out of a faith that he might never have embraced, but it's certainly true that he chose his own way to God: in 1932, at the age of forty, he was confirmed in the Anglican Church of the Resurrection in Bucharest. This was one year after Donald's birth, a long-awaited event that might have turned Joe's mind to higher powers (though it's also possible that he had his stoutly Protestant parents-in-law in mind). The fact that Joe and Elena brought up their children as Anglicans suggests a genuine faith and, if not that, then a cultural attachment to Western, so-called 'Christian' traditions.

As an adult, my father attended church most Sundays. He was on the rota for flower arranging, and he enjoyed hosting the vicar and other parishioners for sherry after the Sunday service. My uncle Peter married an Anglican, and brought his four sons up in the same faith, though he was, and remains, an atheist. My brother Alexander and I were brought up as Catholics, presumably a non-negotiable decision given that my mother came from an English Catholic family who have never been anything else in 1,000 years of continual occupation of the same house. I can't speak for Alexander, or my younger brother, Hugo, but I don't have any religious practice.

So if we're dealing in percentages, nothing here adds up to a clean hundred. In any case I don't want to be the judge, because that's how every identity becomes a potential liability. If we know nothing else, the history of exceptionalism has taught us this. Nor do I want to be bossed around by dead ancestors, innocent or otherwise. I don't want to live with the fretful backward glance, the downward drag of the dead hand on my shoulder. I'd rather be in a place with no mortmain, no past, like Goethe's America, where there are 'no tumbledown castles', and 'inner lives are not disturbed by / Useless memories and vain strife'.

Of course this is a case of wanting things as they never were. We are nothing without the past: it's a form of knowledge, a memorandum of how to survive. We need memory to tool up for life, else how do we learn which is the poison berry, or how to repeat the accident that flies from the flint to start a fire? The problem is too much remembering. How casually we take up the dictum that those who forget history are condemned to repeat it, without considering whether the opposite may be true: that we are doomed to repeat the errors of the past precisely because we can't accept that it is past.

How else to explain the world's many flashpoints, those history-saturated sites where the past continually asserts its rights over the present, where the unforgiving dead rise up to accuse the living and demand revenge? Those contested Balkan shatter zones, for example, whose borders were forever moving back and forth according to the latest exhumation of ancient grievances; places where in peacetime farmers crossed the border to lend each other tools, only to use them to disembowel their neighbours when the ancestral grudge was whipped up again. Why do the dead have rights? And what about those flashpoints within ourselves? It is memory, personal and institutional, that drives the recursive loops of suffering in these places.

Forgetting is not an option. If we only forget, we have no stories, nothing from the past by which to estimate our own lives. Speak, memory. Yes, but tell us things that will not destroy us.

THE RETURN OF THE LIVING

At the end, Hitler's personal *Lebensraum* was a bunker. For Göring, Streicher, Bormann and the others who faced trial in Nuremberg's Palace of Justice, it was beneath the courtroom in six-foot by eight-foot cells, each with an iron bedstead and a begrimed toilet without a seat. The final solution to Germany's demand for living space was to find it underground: cellars, bomb craters, sewers. *Deutschland, Deutschland* unter *alles,* unter *alles in der Welt.*

Above ground, the politics of smash-and-grab were in full reversal. Those Germans who had gone east to take up their place in the new Grossdeutschland found themselves heading back west with nothing to show for it except a few bundles of belongings and, in the case of the Sudeten Germans, the damning distinction of an obligatory yellow armband. In Lower Silesia, south-west Poland, almost two million ethnic Germans were cleared out. Arriving on their heels were Poles from the east, who simply walked into the empty houses and slept between sheets that hours earlier had been warmed by their enemies. When the new arrivals dug their gardens or ploughed their fields, they turned up treasures: porcelain, silk dresses, furs, jewellery, all hastily buried in jars, chests and even coffins by the previous inhabitants, who had themselves found treasure in exactly the same way after they had evicted the previous-previous inhabitants. Everybody was either burying something – valuables, memories, guilt, bodies – or digging something up.

Primo Levi, on returning home to Turin from Auschwitz – a surreally circular five-month journey via Russia (twice) – found in his trouser pocket one of the light alloy coins minted by Chaim Rumkowski. The King of the Łódź ghetto had not escaped the gas chamber, and Levi cashed in this single coin for the following insight: 'Like Rumkowski, we too are so dazzled by power and money as to forget our essential fragility, forget that all of us are in the ghetto, that the ghetto is fenced in, that beyond the fence stand the lords of death, and not far away the train is waiting.'

Levi's own suffering in Auschwitz had been alleviated by Lorenzo Perrone, a bricklayer from Fossano, in northern Italy. As a civilian labourer, Perrone was allowed to receive clothes and food packages from relatives in Italy, but life was still extremely precarious. After a bombing raid in June 1944, he was put on a detail building thick brick walls around the most valuable machines at the huge complex of the Buna Works in Auschwitz. Levi was put on the same detail, ordered to carry buckets of mortar up to the masons on the scaffolding. It was forbidden for civilians and prisoners to speak to each other, but one day Perrone silently handed Levi a piece of bread and his aluminium mess tin with the remainder of his soup ration. Every day for six months he delivered the bread and soup, even after a bomb had fallen close to him and exploded in the soft ground, burying the mess tin and bursting one of his eardrums. The tin was bent out of shape and Perrone muttered that the soup was a bit dirty, without revealing why. In this way, he saved Levi's life.

After the Germans abandoned Auschwitz, Perrone walked out of the gates and, using only a railway map and the stars, piloted himself towards the Brenner Pass. Walking at night, it took him four months to make his way back to Fossano. When Levi returned, he sought Perrone out. He found a tired man, 'not tired from the walk, mortally tired, a weariness without remedy'. His margin of love for life had thinned, almost disappeared. Levi learned that Perrone had been helping other people in Auschwitz, but 'now it was over; he had no more opportunities'.

Levi visited again, bringing Perrone a woollen sweater for the winter. He wanted to 'rescue' Perrone, but he was difficult to reach. The bricklayer had built a high wall around himself and was drinking himself to death.

He had understood many things, but he did not even realize where he had been: Instead of Auschwitz, he used to say Au-Schwiss,* like Switzerland. He was confused in his geography. He couldn't follow a time-table. He would get drunk and sleep in the snow, completely drunk with wine. He got tuberculosis. I sent him to be cured in the hospital. But they did not give him wine, so he escaped. He died of tuberculosis and of alcohol. Yes. It was really suicide.

He was confused in his geography. When Levi was in Auschwitz he had a recurring dream about returning home: it was 'an intense pleasure' to be there and he had many things to recount, but his listeners were 'completely indifferent', talking amongst themselves as if he were not there. When he was finally back home, in Turin, in his own bed, he had another recurring dream: he found himself sitting at a table with his family, everybody was calm and happy, but he sensed a gathering threat, the anguish became 'more intense and more precise', everything around him – the scenery, the walls, the people – collapsed and all was turned to chaos:

I am alone in the centre of a grey and turbid nothing, and now, I know what this thing means, and I also

---

* When Levi was deported from Fossoli in February 1944 there was a sign at the station saying 'Auschwitz', but many of the other Italian prisoners gathered on the platform didn't know what that was; they thought it must have meant Austerlitz, in Bohemia.

*know that I have always known it; I am in the Lager
once more, and nothing is true outside the Lager. All
the rest was a brief pause, a deception of the senses, a
dream; my family, nature in flower, my home. Now
this inner dream, this dream of peace, is over, and in
the outer dream, which continues, gelid, a well-known
voice resounds: a single word, not imperious, but brief
and subdued. It is the dawn command of Auschwitz,
a foreign word, feared and expected: get up, 'Wstawać'.*

There was no home after Auschwitz without Auschwitz
in it.

I've been looking in a yellow wallet-folder I found last
year in my mother's house. It's a mini-archive of the period
just after the war, as experienced through the selective
prism of an English public school, Clifton College in
Bristol, to which Donald and Peter were despatched shortly
after they landed at Liverpool docks. Forged in Romania,
reshaped in the expatriate oasis of Cairo, bent out of shape
in a parochial outpost of South Africa, re-formed again in
Cairo, the Słomnicki boys were finally being properly
anglicised, engineered as true Englishmen, a process that
was so finely calibrated that you would never know they
were anything but.

It took time, of course. Where was that strange name
from? Was that a German accent? If you're English, how
come you can't speak it properly? Gradually the cleft
narrowed between the seasoned refugee who had turned
up like flotsam in England and the public schoolboy who
occupied Study 22 with a chap called Collyns. It never
fully closed, but superficially at least the 'special incom-
pleteness' of the outsider, as V. S. Naipaul described it, was
barely detectable. As Donald came to terms with the split

infinitive ('Napoleon wanted to thoroughly subdue the Iberian Peninsula'), so he found a way to suture the interruptions in his identity.

He worked hard, joined lots of school societies and studied English manners closely (what better laboratory than the game of cricket?). Clifton College gave him structure, order, lines to follow. He lined up in the corridor to file into class, the refectory, chapel; he wrote his test papers in lined notebooks, and underlined all his headings and subheadings twice with a ruler. At the start and end of every term, he filled out the Inventory of Clothes: Pyjamas, 3; Slippers, 1; Socks, prs of, 7; Soft Collars, 2; School Blazer, 1; Cricket Cap; 1. Lines, grids, forms, lists: rules for living that tamed and domesticated the nightmares, boundaries that protected against the nasties beyond.

In Bristol, Donald was closer to the effects of war than he had ever been in Romania or Egypt or South Africa. The city had been heavily bombed, there were craters and piles of rubble everywhere, and those curious vending machines in the train station had not dispensed a Cadbury's chocolate bar for years. With Britain essentially bankrupt, ration coupons for food and clothes provided the most meagre comfort. For all this, Donald was closer to the reassurances of an empire that still spanned a quarter of the globe. In chapel, he prayed to the God whose special task it was to protect this empire – 'God of our fathers, known of old, / Lord of our far-flung battle line, / Beneath whose awful hand we hold / Dominion over palm and pine' – and in his free time he pored over his 1946 Savoy Victory Album, whose pre-printed pages awaited special-issue stamps, assiduously collected, for every British dependency.

The album was confirmation that the war had been won and business as normal could be resumed across an empire that would last indefinitely, every place immutable, in its place. On the opening page, Aden, first occupied by the British in 1839, 'now a great oil bunkering and coaling station and port of call, an emporium for the trade of the adjacent African and Arabian coasts', the caption reads. On the last page, Zanzibar, a British Protectorate since 1890, 'under the administration of H.M. Government through the Governor and Commander-in-Chief in the Kenya Colony and Protectorate'. In between, sixty-five territories, including Australia, Burma, Canada, Ceylon, India, Malaya, New Zealand, Nigeria, Rhodesia, Uganda – all forming 'one family, the wide world over', under King George VI, whose youthful appearance on the stamps belied his rapidly ageing features.

As taught in the classroom, geography was a question of confident global leaps, from the Hampshire basin to the Punjab, the Devon peninsula to the Falkland Islands. The world was studied and mapped as a provider of resources waiting to be extracted by the enterprising British, from the Lancashire cotton industry whose finished goods, Donald wrote in a test paper, 'are sent to all parts of the world, especially the cheap cotton cloths to those parts of Africa and Asia where the natives are becoming "civilised"', to South America with its rubber, copper, sugar, coffee, ivory, nuts, minerals, oil and Panama hats. He was good at drawing maps, and usually got high marks, though in another test paper he shows some confusion over whether the Carpathians were still in Romania: first, he claimed they were 'Now ceeded [sic] to Roumania', then crossed this out. Transylvania, he was sure, was 'Now ceeded to Roumania', while Bessarabia was 'now ceeded to Russia'. It's a muddle, and he dropped a grade.

*

The Carpathians were indeed back in Romania, and Joe Słomnicki was back in the Carpathians. He went straight there after being demobilised from his posting in Tehran in February 1945, joining the Allied Control Commission in Bucharest, tasked with surveying the oil installations that had been bombed by the Allies in 1943 and 1944. His photographs show the extent of the damage: derricks drunkenly skewed at impossible angles; burnt-out, crumpled petroleum tanks; broken segments of elevated pipelines lying in the mud; severed rail tracks rearing up towards the sky from which the bombs had come. Apart from these photographs, there is no other record of Joe's impressions upon returning home.

In late October he was briefly in London to formalise an offer of re-employment with British Petroleum, whose subsidiary, Steaua Romana, he had joined more than twenty years earlier. He was reunited with Helen and the boys, after more than a year of separation, and stayed in a dingy flat near the Thames in Chelsea that Helen had rented. Joe exchanged his first clothing coupons for a suit and an overcoat, to which he added a fedora hat, posing happily in an autumnal garden square with Helen and Donald – now a lanky, ration-thin fourteen-year-old – for a photograph taken by Peter. And then he left again, followed a few months later by Helen.

The plan was to pick up the threads of their former life in Romania. The boys would continue their education at Clifton College, joining their parents in Câmpina during the holidays. They would be at home again, together, in their house, surrounded by their things; and history, that terrible cataract of events that had overwhelmed their lives, would now leave them alone. 'I remember looking out of the window of our sitting room and watching the bench in the garden slowly being covered,' Peter, now eleven, wrote to his parents. 'I hope that when normal times come I will be able to come and see all that we left at such short notice.' It didn't happen – there would be no return to normal times. They looked forward to going back, but when they got there they found that the future was not what it used to be.

When Helen died in 1980 Peter found among her belongings a cardboard shoebox in which she had carefully saved all the letters he had sent her and Joe during his school years. Peter put the shoebox away and forgot about it. It's now on my desk, as are copies of two other primary sources: a Foreign Office file from the National Archives, entitled 'An Account of the Case of Mr Słomnicki', which I discovered by accident while looking for something else in the wrong inventory of the wrong catalogue; and papers from the British Petroleum archive at Warwick University, which I visited a few months ago. Braided together, these three strands form an explanation, in real time, of how the Słomnicki family lost their home for a second time.

> 3 March 1946, Clifton College
> *It must have been very nice to have seen everybody and everything again ... Have you got a wireless yet? What did I look like when I was a baby? ... Can you send me some turkish delight? ... I do hope we will all spend the summer holidays together in Romania.*

Helen has recently arrived in Romania. She has been in Câmpina, staying with her sister Marta, who still calls her Elena. For some reason she and Joe have not moved back into their own house, instead renting a flat in Bucharest. As under-manager and chief geologist of Steaua Romana, Joe is often away in the company's headquarters in Ploieşti.

10 March 1946, Clifton College
As you know, Donald was confirmed. It was a very nice service and Donald looked most smart walking up. I do not know how he felt ... Do you think you could get a Roumanian Grammar from anywhere? I have forgotten almost every word, and want to learn again.

23 June 1946, Clifton College
It is a great pity about the situation in Roumania. I hope we __will__ be able to come in the end ... On Friday afternoon Winston Churchill drove through Clifton College. We all watched him. He was in a large open car with his cigar, his bowler hat, and the V sign as usual. Yesterday the boy who won a scholarship gave a feast. We had sosage [sic] rolls, trifle, lemonade, strawberry and ice cream.

General Antonescu, who took Romania into Hitler's war against the Soviet Union, has been executed for treason and war crimes. King Michael still occupies the throne, but Stalinists are running the country. The old constitution is torn up and replaced, all rights to freedom of speech and political association are removed. No Romanian is allowed to leave the country without authority. Romania, the first country to be 'liberated' by the Soviet Union, is now a prison.

14 July 1946, Clifton College
Have you heard any more about the summer holidays? Have you had any more news about getting a Ford? I hope this will be possible.

28 July 1946, Clifton College
This is the last day of term and there is great excitment [sic] in the house. Yesterday evening we had a

cinema show. Then we had a swim, and a feast of
jelly, cake, ice cream, oranges, and milk.... Do you
think you will be able to do anything about the
Christmas holidays? I am afraid it is looking rather
far ahead, but I hope the peace conference will help
matters over Roumania. I will take care to write every
Sunday in the holidays and not neglect it as I did last
holidays.

The plan for Donald and Peter to spend the summer in
Romania has come to nothing. Instead they stay at the Old
Manor, Dunster, a boarding house in Somerset run by the
thoroughly arthritic Mrs Bland. Peace negotiations formalise the restoration of Transylvania to Romania from
Hungary, and the other provinces lost in 1940 are awarded
to the Soviet Union and Bulgaria.

9 February 1947, Clifton College
How are you both? ... I wonder if it is very cold and
if you are having very much snow in Roumania. I
certainly hope, Mummy, that you will not fall ill again.
Have you had any more news about Donald and I
coming over to see you in the summer holidays? I
certainly hope that this will be possible.

The coldest winter in Europe on record – nature's over-
ture to the frozen topography of the Cold War.

4 May 1947, Clifton College
Are you sure about summer hols yet?

29 May 1947, Clifton College
I will be taking some music out to Roumania when I
come and I will certainly bring my tennis racket.

After so much uncertainty, Donald and Peter finally get back to Romania, spending the summer in their aunt Marta's house in Câmpina with her daughters, Rodica and Sanda, both now married. They visit their own house, which has been damaged by an earthquake, and go through some of their possessions. Joe has a new car and they tour their favourite places, hiking in the Carpathians and staying for some days at the summer villa of Prince Ştirbei in Braşov.

In the middle of the holiday Joe's friend and colleague, Vlad Eker, is 'purged' from his job at Steaua by the 'Red' trades union as a 'lackey of capitalism'. His bosses, who include Joe, continue to pay Vlad's salary *sub rosa*, handing it to him in cash at the company's office in Bucharest. Similar payments are made, off the books, to other purged employees. Alexander Evans, the managing director, enters details of every payment in code in his pocket notebook.

In late September the boys return to school.

28 September 1947, Clifton College
I will relate my adventures from when I left you at the airport [in Bucharest]. I got into the 'plane prepared for a good flight. We took off safely and it was smooth for some time. <u>But</u> when we got over the Carpathians we encountered a storm. We took an extra hour trying to get round it but from then till the end of the journey the plane went like this [zigzag diagram] *and so on. I, of course was very sick. They supplied paper bags, thank goodness!! When we landed [in Vienna] I was quite exhausted but we had a cup of hot tea and then went to Hotel Astoria ... The next morning we went to find if our papers were O.K. they were and then we saw the zoo. In the evening we went to a cinema and then to the station. our sleeper had broken down!!!!!!!!!!!!! We got into*

*a compartement [and] I slept from 12:30–3:00 and
3:30–7:00 about in a most uncomfortable sitting position! ... We got to Basle at about 6:00 and changed
trains and got various things on the station: Nescafe
(which we will send soon), chocolate and fruit ...
When we got to London we got a taxi and went to
Paddington at 5:45 to find that we had missed the
5:30 and had to wait till 7:30! We eventually got to
Bristol at 11:00.*

31 October 1947, Clifton College
*I hope you can get the silver and rugs off soon. I am
pleased to hear you have curtains but if you hope to
come here soon was it worth getting them made I
suppose it was. I am in perfect health and have not
had any colds. I hope it is the same with you. All my
very best love and many many kisses, Peter.*

The rapid Sovietisation of Romania has forced their hand:
Joe and Helen start shipping their belongings to England,
sending the most precious items first.

On 30 December 1947 King Michael is forced to abdicate.
That evening, in a rigged meeting of Parliament, the
monarchy is abolished and replaced by the Romanian
People's Republic. Speed being an essential element in any
heist, only forty-five minutes are allowed for the whole
proceeding, of which twenty minutes are devoted to
ovations and applause. The following morning, Michael
Hohenzollern leaves by train for Switzerland, to take up
his place among the exiled grandees of Europe.

17 January 1948, Weybridge, c/o Redgraves
*I certainly hope that this New Year will bring us
together very soon ... Easter here is very early this*

*year: 28th MARCH! I hope you will both be settled here
before then. All my best love and a billion kisses, Peter.*

Robin and Micheline Redgrave are safe, if penniless, in
England with their daughters. Donald and Peter sometimes
stay with them in the holidays. They see very little of Roy,
who is now rising in the ranks of the Royal Household
Guard, having joined in late 1944, shortly after his nine-
teenth birthday. In the very last days of the war, while he
was leading a scouting party near the River Oste, west of
Hamburg, a German rocket had hit his armoured car. He
was behind the car at the time, taking a piss on the rear
wheel, but in two bounds he was on the engine cover,
dragging his gunner out of the smoking turret. Despite
being wounded under fire, he saved the gunner, earning
himself the Military Cross.

8 February 1948, Clifton College
*Daddy, I think that you will never be able to get a
Re-entry visa so please use the exit one if you have it.
I am sure such a clever Poppa as I have <u>must</u> be able
to get a job here!! … at long last, the crate has arrived.
I am very pleased that it was not lost and also that
my accordion was in it.*

The huge shipping crate contains everything Joe and
Helen could squeeze into it. The rest of their possessions
they have either sold or given away. Joe's exit permit has
expired and he is trying to get it renewed. He is under
surveillance by the secret police. Every aspect of Romania's
political and social structure is now targeted by the *Siguranţa*
(to be replaced in August by the *Securitate*). Thousands of
citizens are arrested without charge, tortured and deported
to labour camps as 'a danger to society'. Romanians replace

normal conversation with coded messages or parables. Or silence.

3 March 1948, Clifton College
The news that you will be here in June is the best I have had since I knew I was going to you last summer, and it is even better than that because I now know that I will, at last, have a home in England. I will leave it to Donald to write to Mrs Bland about Easter as he always arranges these things.

On the night of 3 March, George Moriatti, director-general of Steaua Romana, a Romanian national, flees the country along with his wife and sister-in-law. A week earlier he had authorised a large withdrawal of Steaua funds to finance his escape. Alexander Evans signed off the transfer and Joe countersigned, apparently innocent of its purpose.

8 April 1948, Old Manor, Dunster
Mummy, I am very pleased that you will, I hope, be here so soon but at the same time I am very sorry that you, Daddy, will have to stay on a bit longer. Still, I suppose it is all to the good as you will still have your job ... I hope you will both hurry and come and get a house so till my next letter or till I see you I send you all my very best love and lots of kisses, Peter.

22 April 1948, Old Manor, Dunster
This letter is, I hope, mainly for you, Daddy, as I hope Mummy will be here having left before this letter arrives. If she has, <u>please</u> hurry and follow her. Thank you very much for the letters we received this morning of the 12th and 15th containing all the stamps for Donald. He has catalogued some of them and has

already found 2 of £12 each if they are not forgeries!
He thinks that the whole lot may be worth about £50!!
Donald and some friends are going to cycle to Cheddar
and back tomorrow, 40 miles each way. Only 3 days
of the holidays left now. Time has absolutely flown
past. Anyhow I hope it will be the last 3 days of holi-
days I will ever spend without you.

Sometime between this letter and the next, Helen leaves Bucharest by the newly resumed but distinctly shabby Orient Express. Since Moriatti's escape, wives of the imperialist jackals 'stealing oil from the state-owned subsoil' are being watched. When the train reaches Curtici, at the border with Hungary, plain-clothes police take Helen off and search her luggage. By the time they've finished, the train has left. She waits, alone and terrified, for another service to take her out of the country. She eventually makes her way back to London, and to the gloomy flat in Chelsea.

By early June, Joe is aware that the state-installed administrator of Steaua Romana, a known communist, is reporting directly to the *Siguranţa*.

6 June 1948, Clifton College
Dear Mummy, I sincerely hope Daddy <u>will</u> be here
on the 15th so that I will see him at commemoration
... You made a very wise decision about houses and
the important thing now is to get a furnished flat in
time for next holidays. You must think 'A Matter of
Life and Death' very good to see it 3 times! ... I am
anxiously awaiting more news from you.

On 7 June, Alexander Evans leaves Bucharest at 23.10 on the Orient Express, for consultations with head office in London. His passport and exit visa are in order. He takes his notebook with him.

10 June 1948, Clifton College
Dear Mummy, I am enclosing a pair of pyjamas. There is a huge rip in the seat of the trousers. I do not want to trust it to the matron so I am sending it to you. Could you please wash and mend it and send it back to me? ... I am expecting you to tell me that Daddy has arrived in your next letter so till then I send you all my very best love and kisses, Peter.

Helen is anxious to hear from Joe. Is it possible he has tried to leave the country without an exit visa? On 11 June the British Legation in Bucharest receives a telegram from an eye-witness claiming that at 1 p.m. on 8 June Alexander Evans was taken off the train at the border by three plain-clothes officers. Consular enquiries are met with a wall of silence. Romanian industry, banking, insurance, oil, mining and transport are nationalised. Joe no longer has a job.

On 16 June, nine days after Evans's disappearance, it is confirmed that he has been arrested and is being held at the Interior Ministry for questioning. His notebook with the coded entries is in the hands of the police, and they now want to pull Joe in. They go to Joe's flat but he isn't there, having taken refuge in the British Consul's residence. It is feared that 'If Mr Slomnicki were to leave the consul's house he would almost certainly be arrested by the police agents on watch there.'

Evans is formally charged with fraudulent use of Steaua Romana's funds. On the morning of 1 July, Joe, accompanied by a legation official, goes to the tribunal dealing with the case to make a deposition. He is immediately arrested and taken for questioning about an accusation brought against him in relation to the alleged fraud. The consul intervenes and, 'after 24 hours of stormy interviews with everybody concerned', obtains Joe's release with the guarantee that he will not leave the country.

3 July 1948, Clifton College
Dear Mummy, I am just scribbling a few words to ask you to send as soon as possible a note saying that I am allowed to go down a coal mine next Tuesday. Don't worry, it is not dangerous so please send it as quickly as possible to get here by Tuesday ... Have you had news from Daddy?

Now released, Joe has returned to his flat. His line is tapped, telegrams are unsafe, as are letters, unless sent via the legation in the diplomatic bag. For one week Helen is unaware of his whereabouts. News of the Evans arrest having been widely broadcast in the British media, including the BBC, she fears the worst.

9 July 1948, Clifton College
Dear Mummy, Thank goodness Daddy is safe back in the [Bucharest] flat now. I hope this idea of a collective visa for all oil men works out! ... I am so pleased you did manage to get a cottage for the holidays. Has it a nice garden? How many rooms, etc.? Please send all particulars. Also I hope the rent is not as much as that awful place in Chelsea! ... Please keep writing and telling me of any further news of Daddy.

The Evans trial opens on this day. It is held at the *Prefectura*, in 'a dirty, noisy, shoddy little court-room in which thieves, drunkards, prostitutes and other dregs of the Bucharest population are normally tried'. Evans is brought to the court in a lorry with other prisoners, then taken back to the verminous Văcăreşti prison, where he shares a cell with seventy other men. Unlike them, he is spared the repeated interrogations, accompanied by 'the crudest forms of torture', that take place in the middle of the night. Over the next three months Joe regularly takes food to the prison for Evans.

On 25 August 1948 the Associated Press reports that 'two Britons and several Roumanians are to face trial at Bucharest on charges of misusing National Bank credits granted to the oil companies for which they worked, it was officially announced last night. The Britons are Alexander Evans and Joe Flomniki [*sic*], who will face charges brought against them as managers of ... Steaua Romana.'

26 August 1948, Llanishen, nr Cardiff
Dear Mummy, If Daddy does not get out in the very near future I am going to steal a helicopter and fly there and rescue him!

On 23 September 1948 the legation telegraphs the Foreign Office that the 'Evans case is not going well and may end in a grave denial of justice in which Slomnicki may be involved'.

28 September 1948, Clifton College
Daddy must be pretty fed up if he does not even mind where he lives! So are we. Why can't he pinch a plane and fly away? ... I am so pleased you have managed to find some rooms for you and Daddy, so that you can start house-searching from there.

17 October 1948, Clifton College
*Thank goodness that letter from Daddy did eventually
arrive! But did you see today's Sunday Times about
Evans!!! 4,9000,000 lei to Steaua, 4,000 damages and
900 fined ± 3 YEARS. The grossest injustice ever. Of
course he lodged an appeal. Is it not awful! ... I have
just gone to Clifton, cashed the £1, and got a pot of
plum jam, off the ration.*

16 November 1948, Clifton College
*I am so pleased you have got somewhere for us next
holidays and if Daddy is not there with us I will get
so annoyed, that I will —, well I don't know what I
will do! How big is the house? What's it like? Please
tell me all about it ... Tomorrow there is a whole
holiday for the school because of the birth of a boy to
Princess Elizabeth.*

The same day the legation reports to the Foreign Office
that 'Since June Mr Slomnicki has remained in Bucharest
in constant fear of arrest, spending most of his time on
Legation premises. This life is beginning to tell on him,
and he has recently shown signs of nervousness and dissat-
isfaction with what is being done on his behalf.' It is agreed
that Joe's 'position is intolerable, and has been so for
months', that 'the time has clearly come for something
drastic to be done', but the Foreign Office is keen to avoid
the 'strong possibility that an awkward Parliamentary
Question may soon be asked on behalf of Mrs Slomnicki'.
The problem is, as all parties know, that Evans is guilty as
charged, and so is Joe.

On 20 November Evans is released on bail at midday,
pending appeal. Bail is set at £26,000 (£600,000 in today's

value) and is paid by the Foreign Office, though the sum has in fact been raised by Steaua Romana in London, which 'do not wish their name to be associated with the transaction lest their shareholders accuse them of compounding a felony'. Basically, this is a get-out-of-jail bribe, the plan being to spirit Evans out of the country as soon as possible. The case against Joe has stalled and 'it remains a matter of urgency to get him out [before] the Roumanians have more time to [prepare other] charges'.

25 November 1948, Clifton College
In exactly one month's time from now it will be Xmas day and if Daddy is not with us then! I'll break the neck of every Russian or Communist I see ... About my wishes I would not mind some odd records or maybe an exposure meter for my photography, or I would not mind a new car, or a home, or a room of my own, or a nice wireless, or lots of things, but most are impossible!

Joe did get back in time for Christmas. After much haggling, including the threat to block the sale of tractors to Romania, the Foreign Office prevailed. He was granted an exit visa on Thursday, 9 December 1948, and booked a flight to Prague for the Saturday, but at the last minute the flight was suspended due to bad weather. He raced to the station, got on a train, passed the border – no doubt in a state of acute anxiety, and with barely a suitcase – and a few days later he was in London. He never spoke to his sons about the affair, except to say that he had spent one night in prison and that was more than enough.

As for Evans, the hearing of his appeal being endlessly delayed, on 22 January 1949 he was given an exit visa (and a re-entry visa, should he be stupid enough to return for the verdict). He left the country that day. A week later his appeal was rejected. George Moriatti, who, it turns out, had links to British intelligence, was sentenced *in absentia* to five years. Most of Joe's Romanian colleagues were put up in show trials or simply disappeared. Mircea Cancicov, the chairman of the Steaua Romana Board from 1941 until 1947, and Istrate Micescu, a commercial lawyer who had handled work for the company, were both sentenced to twenty-five years, to be served in the notorious prison complex of Aiud, in Transylvania. Micescu, who was seventy, survived only two years.

There is a coda. Vlad Eker, Joe's colleague who had been supported with secret cash payments after he had been purged, attempted by various means to escape from the country, with the result that, just before Christmas 1953, he was arrested and 'interrogated' for six months in a basement of the *Securitate* in Ploieşti. Charged with treason, economic sabotage and attempting to leave the country illegally, he was sentenced to two years. During his trial, evidence was produced of the illicit payments he had received from the 'convicted' criminal Joseph Słomnicki. Joe himself, traded for tractors, was indeed found guilty, *in absentia*, for his part in the Steaua Romana fraud. I don't know how many years he was sentenced to, only that he didn't serve them. Better out of Romania than dead, as the saying went.

A scrap of newspaper, brown with age, is being carefully unfolded in the palm of someone's hand. Who? Where are we? A room with windows to our backs, an open door ahead, and beyond that a wall with a long diagonal crack in the plaster. My father is here, and my brother Alexander, but this is not our house. Somebody is handing the scrap to my father. They are talking about it – I don't know what it says. Something to do with Daddy's father? A bad thing. I am distracted; someone is holding a glass of white wine, but when it's turned upside-down the wine doesn't fall out.

It wasn't a dream, but a memory, albeit one I had attached to the wrong crisis. It's been knocking around in my head like a bluebottle and now it's finally out. It's April 1977, and we are in the house of Granny Helen's sister, Marta, in Câmpina. The wall is cracked because of a recent earthquake, and the wine glass is a trick performed by Tudor, Marta's grandson – he offers it to me, pretends to stumble and the glass tips over but, instead of spilling, the wine magically disappears. Tudor has found it in the attic while searching for the newspaper cutting. The article is in Romanian, but Daddy's ability to understand any language other than English has been lost, like Eeyore's tail, so Marta's daughter, Sanda, is translating it for him: 'Joseph Słomnicki ... Steaua Romana ... economic saboteur ... enemy of the People's Republic of Romania ... sentenced to ... years in prison.'

Daddy is leaning over the article as Sanda reads, and when she stops, he takes a step back and blinks several times. He looks like he has eaten ashes. Tudor takes the article back to the attic along with the wine glass, while we go downstairs to be with Granny Helen and Tante Marta. Granny has something called hardening of the arteries, which always makes me think of traffic jams, and she is sitting in the porch asking, in German, for her sister – 'Where is Marta? Where is Marta?' – while Marta, who is sitting next to her, gently strokes her hand.

Helen's return to Romania was as disorienting as her previous departures: the first under the eyes of German soldiers in October 1940, the second under the eyes of Stalinist secret police in the spring of 1948. By the time of our visit in 1977 she was already lost in dementia, a stranger in her own midst. She did not recognise the house she had shared with Joe, the house where her children had played, with the garden full of tulips and the climbing pole and swing; the house where her widowed mother had lived on the top floor, staying on after Joe and Helen and the boys had fled to Istanbul, and cowering one night under her eiderdown, rubble falling around her, as a massive earthquake brought down the ceiling in the boys' bedroom; the house where she had died in late 1943, the news delivered to a distraught Helen in Cairo; the house that had long since been expropriated by the communists and turned into a municipal library.

For the greater part of our visit, Helen was somewhere very distant behind a vacant stare. Her sister and nieces loved her with the quiet, simple confidence that she might yet be able to receive some comfort, and a couple of times she did actually recognise them, with the kind of astonishment of someone who finds herself surrounded by guests at a surprise birthday party, only to forget immediately afterwards who they are. For my father it was a great strain, and he couldn't wait to get away, so we left for a week of touring his favourite childhood places in a rented Dacia with a back seat that levitated every time we hit a bump in the road.

We went to Poiana, in the mountains of Brașov, and tried to ski on the last patch of snow. We found the holiday cottage Joe had bought, which had been requisitioned as a first-aid post, so we walked in and Daddy told the indifferent receptionist that this was his father's house and that (pointing) was his tiled stove. We took long walks in the ancient forests, following shepherds' tracks up to the high meadows, and there, alone among the numberless multitude of wild flowers, we laid out a picnic of whatever food we had found in the almost-empty shops, washed down with something optimistically labelled as orange juice: a flavoured powder mixed with sorbic acid. You had to shake the bottle to bring the contents together, and it brought on a fierce thirst that sent us looking for the nearest stream, Daddy scooping up the water so that we could drink from his cupped hands.

We bounced along in the Dacia to Bran Castle, home, or so we believed, of Vlad the Impaler, better known as Dracula. At the entrance we were told to remove our shoes and step into fluffy cotton slippers, so as not to scratch the polished stone floors. We shuffled into the sepulchral silence of the fortress, the temperature dropping as we moved from the outer halls to the interior rooms. When Daddy whispered, 'How would you like your *stake*? Rare, medium, or through-and-through?' we collapsed in giggles. It was a rare joke.

There was nothing in the museum guide about the castle having belonged to Queen Marie, or that the casket containing her heart had been interred in the chapel since 1940, brought here from her summer residence in southern Dobruja just days before it was lost to Bulgaria. Her daughter Ileana had it placed in a marble sarcophagus and cemented it in so firmly that when she had to flee the country after the monarchy was abolished, she couldn't get it out again. It stayed at Bran until the regime desecrated the chapel in 1971, whereafter it was put it in a storeroom at the National History Museum in Bucharest. (It remained there until November 2015, when, after a seventy-seven-year journey around the country, it was taken by Marie's descendants back to her Carpathian palace and placed in the room in which she had died.)

We returned to Câmpina with our stories. Daddy was less impatient with his mother now, even learning to ignore her habit of taking her false teeth out and placing them in the nearest cup of tea. We all adjusted to the oddities, including her request to see her mother, who had been dead for more than thirty years. There we were, in a broken country with a broken woman who couldn't put the pieces together again, but we were together and we were happy.

There was a large covered balcony at Tante Marta's house, and we spent a lot of time under its shadow in the afternoons. It was there that Marta's older daughter, Rodica, handed my father a handkerchief in which were wrapped three gold Napoleonic coins. She explained that she had hidden the coins in the autumn of 1940, when the Germans occupied the nearby oilfields. She had cycled to the woods, dug a hole under a tree and buried the coins along with a few other valuables. After the war she went back to dig them up, but the trees had grown and it took her hours to find the spot. Shortly after the coup that unseated King Michael in 1947, she hid them again and now, she said, she wanted Daddy to have them. He protested, but Rodica insisted: she was too scared to hold on to them because ownership of any foreign currency was illegal under Ceaușescu's dictatorship. Daddy eventually relented, saying he would keep the coins safe for her. When we packed to leave for the airport, he tied them into a knot in his handkerchief, which he put in his pocket. We had to go through a metal detector at the airport but fortunately, like everything else, it was broken and we passed through without any trouble. Rodica is long since gone, but my younger brother, Hugo, has the coins in safekeeping.

One evening at Tante Marta's house, my brother Alexander said he had a runny tummy. It soon developed into acute diarrhoea, and he spent most of that night and the following day on the loo. Communist Romania had no money for loo paper (it didn't even have money for money, hence the filthy over-circulated banknotes and shortage of coins), so our cousins made their own from torn-up squares of newspaper (studiously unread), which dangled from a wire. The object was to shit on Comrade Ceauşescu's face, but to everyone's delight, Alexander distinguished himself by running through the entire *nomenklatura*.

There was a law forbidding any foreigner except for a relative in the first degree to stay in a Romanian home. Helen, as Marta's sister, could and did stay in her house. As Marta's nephew, Daddy could also have stayed there, but Alexander and I could not, so he had taken a room for the three of us at a nearby hotel. Every night, after brushing our teeth, we would plant a blob of toothpaste in the middle of the bathroom mirror, to obscure the gaze of the secret policeman who, we were convinced, was spying on us from the other side. We were the only guests in the hotel (it felt like we were the only tourists in the whole of Romania), but there were always several men in hideous oversized suits hanging around in the silent lobby.

Many years later Sanda told me that soon after we flew back to England she had been called in by the local *Securitate*. During the interview they asked her to explain Alexander's illegal overnight stay. They also knew about the salami we had given them (Daddy had paid a substantial bribe to obtain it from the hotel's cook, and we bore it triumphantly to our last meal together in Tante Marta's house). I was appalled by Sanda's revelation and apologised profusely for causing her trouble. She laughed, said that by then she was no longer scared and had told the *Securitate* goons that she knew who they were – she was old enough to be their mother and remembered them in shorts.

She also told me that her ambition had been to become a doctor, and as a young medical student in the war she had amputated a man's leg after a British bombing raid on the oil refineries in Câmpina. She was given a little saw and told to get on with it. I said that must have been terrifying. 'No, no,' she answered brightly, 'I enjoyed it, I knew it was something I was good at. But the *Securitate* knew that Joe Slomnicki was my uncle – they reminded me of this every time they called me in – and they blocked my way, so I had to settle with being a dentist instead. They were stupid, no? They lost a good doctor.'

Whatever their private sorrows or humiliations, Tante Marta and her family faced the awful world in which they lived with incredible dignity. I loved their subversive *esprit*, I loved their love for each other, I loved being with them – I felt at home.

Three years after this visit, on New Year's Eve 1980, Elena-Helen Hotz-Hotti-Słomnicki-Saunders died. A few days earlier Daddy took us to see her in the care home. She was in bed, very weak, but able to raise her arm to admire her bracelet and mutter something in German. She was dying in a language we could not understand. Maybe she was trying to tell us the story of the bracelet: that it was given to her as surety when she and Marta fled the German invasion of Romania in 1916, and that she managed to hold on to it through every twist and turn thereafter. I truly believe that, as she turned the blue plastic beads on their nylon thread, she saw and felt the gold bracelet on her wrist.

Nostalgia settles on a lie, it's how we cope with reality. Helen had it in spades, but I never felt that Daddy was possessed by it as she was. His version of nostalgia was more like a creature that appears every now and then, leaves its scent and slopes off again. From a distance, he regarded his childhood home with affection, but he did not strain to re-create it. A house is a house is a house; what makes it a home is imagination. It's the same with countries, and it's the same with families: we make them up. My father's problem was not that he was trying to sustain an earlier fantasy – of belonging, of recognising and being recognised – but that he wasn't capable of making a new one.

So many houses, none of them home. After Joe's escape from Romania, there was a rental in Woodspring Road, Surrey. Here they took on a Mrs Saunders as a cleaner. Was it a coincidence that Saunders was the name taken by deed poll, in January 1949, when 'Joseph George Saunders, a naturalised British subject renounced and abandoned on behalf of himself, his wife and children and remoter issue the surname of Slomnicki'? 'I'm not sure,' says Peter, 'but it had to start with an "S" because that was the initial engraved on the family silver.'

Next came Brickfield Farm in Sussex, purchased with Joe's one-off payment from Steaua Romana ('in recognition of his loyal service under arduous, difficult and sometimes dangerous conditions'). It was here that they unpacked the crate that had been sent from Câmpina in early 1948, and the crate itself they used as a garage for Joe's new car. They set up as poultry farmers, the boys pitching in during the school holidays to install fencing and coops and incubators and whatever else it takes to make an egg. Former king Michael Hohenzollern was doing the same in Hertfordshire, but with more success: Joe and Helen made a loss, despite Robin Redgrave's help, and gave it and the house up when they moved to Papua New Guinea, where Joe prospected for oil and Helen, finding herself in the middle of a steaming jungle, far away from far away, had a meltdown.

When they returned a year later they bought a house at 25 Green Lane, Purley, Surrey. Donald had started National

Service and Peter was still at boarding school, trying to visualise the new house:

Is it old, new, like the rest in the road, warm, cold, high, low, good floors, draught-proof windows, attic, shed in garden, big or small garage???? We might be able to use those lovely brass chandeliers from Roumania with a bit of alteration for the different English bulbs. From the plan of the house it looks to me as if it would be possible if we were to stay in the house for some time to bash a large door with a sliding or folding door between what will be the sitting-room and Daddy's study, like in Roumania.

Purley was not like Romania – nothing was. And no, there wasn't time to bash a wall out, because Joe was offered work in Canada, so off he went to Calgary with Helen, who developed tonsillitis and a thyroid problem, for which she had to be treated with a very expensive radioactive drink. And so it went on, the *Wanderjahre* of necessity, the incompatibility of light bulbs, until Joe died in England in November 1966, aged seventy-three. He had become a man of few words, there being, perhaps, too much that could be said. Shortly after his death, Peter found a piece of paper on a table by his father's bedside, on which he had begun to scratch out the words of the Lord's Prayer.

Donald was thirty-five, married with two very young children and pursuing a successful career as an economist for a merchant bank. He had shared the first nine years of his life with his father, and then came the night when the steamer put out from the port of Constanţa, carrying the family away from their home and from each other. Over the twenty-six years that followed, the time Donald spent with Joe can be counted as a matter of months. They became strangers to each other. How could it be otherwise?

I don't remember anything about my grandfather (I was barely six months old when he died), but when I look at photographs of him in his later years – unsmiling, detached – I can't help thinking of T. S. Eliot's hollow men surveying the dead land.

HOW TO GET INTO MY FATHER'S HOUSE

Get out of the car, take your bag from the boot, walk to an opening with no door and stand under the lintel. Wait as Daddy goes in and gropes in the dark for a set of keys, which are hidden on top of the oil tank, along with a torch. Once the torch is on, try to ignore the sight of cobwebs slung like fishing nets – concentrate instead on Daddy as he unlocks a door immediately to your right. This door leads into a large utility room with a bare cement floor. Enter behind Daddy, wait for him to turn off the torch and switch on the strip light, which hums and flickers as if it has forgotten its purpose, then proceed straight across the room and up a few steps to another door. Wait as Daddy turns a different key in this lock, then enter the long galley kitchen, at the end of which, on the right, is a door that swings two ways. Wait with your bag while Daddy disappears through it into the room beyond, where the alarm is. When the beeps stop, follow him into the next room and turn left through a door that gives onto the sitting room and the house proper.

My childhood was a study of the register of closing doors. When slammed, the front door of our house in West London (the one we all lived in, until suddenly we didn't) returned a sonic boom that shook the whole house. The door in the kitchen of Daddy's house swished back and forth with a pneumatic sigh and was therefore not good for slamming, though he did try it once or twice. The door of my bedroom had a latch that closed with a snap, though I preferred to keep it open at night, so I could see the light coming from underneath Daddy's bedroom door at the end of the landing. This door was very odd, the previous owners having strapped a mattress to it. It closed with a kind of squishy thump, and it was very hard for a child to open, but I don't think Daddy had any intention of keeping us out; it was just that this was the door as he found it.

I don't understand why my memory falls so stubbornly on the unhomeliness of Daddy's house. The forbidding ritual of crossing dark thresholds, the hollowness of a house only lived in at weekends (until he remarried he worked in London, using a rented flat during the week), the gaps between the tins of food in the kitchen cupboards – all this did make for a rather desultory experience, yet I seem to have privileged this feeling over other feelings, as if the home I'm most comfortable remembering is the one where there was the least comfort, like the armchair with the collapsed springs that's now in my brother Hugo's flat.

That chair wasn't always broken, and being in my father's house was not as depressing as I like to fancy. It's as if I have chosen to fatten my grief with grievance – the memory of Daddy's back as he mowed the lawn (turning his back on *me*) – rather than selecting from other images, such as his delight when I finally landed the ping-pong ball on his side of the table; or in raising a clod of earth to show me a nest of baby rabbits (he gently replaced it and stopped digging that border); in unlocking the mystery of cooking frozen peas (no more 'bullets'); in turning over the treasures I found with my metal detector (one fork and a chunk of iron ore) or the fossils I picked out of the chalk gravel;

in seeing me make my first, precarious loop of the garden on my bicycle, without stabilisers.

I don't have the list Daddy made of his best childhood memories, the one he showed me that day when I was doing the washing-up after lunch. I have long nurtured the hope that it might be in the suitcase. But why should I go looking for it, if I can substitute it with a list of my own?

* Filling punnets with the season's first strawberries at a nearby pick-your-own farm
* Picking wild blueberries in the hills above Cheddar Gorge
* Sitting together on the wicker sofa watching *Dr Who*, Alexander and I deliciously spooked by the psychedelic opening credits; and *Dad's Army* (yeah, 'Who do you think you are kidding, Mr Hitler?' Mr Hitler, who's only got one ball, the other is in the Albert Hall)
* Fetching the box of decorations from the attic and untangling miles of Christmas lights
* Lying in front of the fireplace looking in the flames for 'pictures'
* Preparing our suitcases for a skiing holiday
* Eating oranges and Kendal Mint Cake high up on a mountain, our skis planted in the snow next to us
* Flying kites on the top of Silbury Hill with Roy and Valerie Redgrave and their sons, Robin and Alexander, then whizzing down its steep grassy sides on sheets of cardboard.

The problem, I now see, is not that there was no happiness, but that it retreated so quickly – a function of our necessarily short stays with Daddy (weekends and occasionally a week, rarely more), but also of his recessive nature. He could withdraw into himself very quickly, and this produced an awkwardness – as in 'turned in the wrong direction' – that was hard to correct. He did not oppose his own unhappiness, so I tried to eclipse it with a tungsten flare. He called me 'Sparkles', and for a while I enjoyed the power of making his eyes light up, but it was a deception, a false self, and eventually I got tired of it. As I entered my teenage years the voltage dropped and I began to meet his withdrawals with my own. Schooled in disappointment, he reached for more, once saying, in front of Alexander and me, that a friend of his had recently announced it was better to expect nothing from your children; that way they couldn't let you down. In my head, I replied, 'Be careful what you wish for.'

It was in the mountains that Daddy seemed most at home with himself. If he went to ski, he took us with him; if he went to trek or climb, he didn't. He was an experienced mountaineer, with recorded climbs in the Alps, the Canadian Rockies and the Himalayas. He understood pitons, ropes, carabiners and belays, and his kit included crampons (they looked like animal traps) and a pickaxe for climbing ice-walls. He had no fear of clinging to a rock face, even after a near-fatal fall in Canada in his twenties, which tore the clothes off his back and most of the skin off one forearm, for which he had to have a skin graft. Odd as it sounds, I think that dangling on a rope over a sheer drop offered him an early freedom from insecurity, a sublime moment of reprieve before the false floor of his own reality opened up again.

I've always wondered whether the course of his descent into dementia was entirely passive. It's not that I believe he colluded with Alzheimer's – like every disease, it has a mind of its own – but that, at some unconscious level, he may have been relieved to accept the offer of an exit from himself, of cutting the rope so as not to have to deal with any further disappointments. The angle of his decline grew steeper and steeper and then he just plunged into the nowhere below. Physically he survived for three, four years (was it more?), but it was as if his life had already passed and he was leading a posthumous existence while still in his body.

All this time I've been asking where did he come from, when perhaps what I really meant to ask was: where did he go? He was so often not there, even when he was. I had no power to stop him going, and then he really left, for good. Sometimes, in my dreams, he reappears looking well, and he is puzzled that we are surprised to see him. *Was it all a mistake? We thought you had lost your mind. And then you died. No?* He is smiling. He doesn't know what we're referring to. He goes off to do some gardening.

RETURN OF THE DEAD

When he was alive, Daddy was never so present to me as he has been in death. Anton Chekhov suggested that 'every happy man should have an unhappy man, in his closet, with a hammer, to remind him with his constant tapping, that not everyone is happy'. Daddy is the man in the closet. Tap-tap-tap. Why does he haunt me? *Why this mad desire to get back to the light?*

Or could it be that I am haunting him? Here I am, sitting at my kitchen table, surrounded by remnants of his life – documents, stamp albums, photographs, the two sixpences I found all those years ago when we were throwing his National Service uniform into the skip – demanding that he answer my questions. What's the difference between this and Queen Victoria laying a place at the table for her Albert and draping his clothes over the chair? Or those Victorian memento-mori photographs of the dead in full dress, doing everyday things like reading a book, as if they were alive? Which, paradoxically, was almost the case, because in the early days of slow-exposure photography the dead performed much better than the living: they kept absolutely still (with the help of hidden supports), whereas the living couldn't hold their breath for long and tended to move slightly, which made them a bit blurred, ghostly.

Why can't we allow the dead to be dead? C. S. Lewis remembers vaguely 'all sorts of ballads and folk tales in which the dead tell us that our mourning does them some kind of wrong. They beg us to stop it.' *What possesses the poor souls?* We do. It is we who keep them at our beck and call, not the other way round. In my dreams, Daddy is riding the Piccadilly Line or doing the gardening because I have put him there. In my waking hours, as I search for a gap in the fence or a hole in the wire, Daddy is required to be there when I have wriggled through to the other side.

There is no border crossing that will take me to my father, because he doesn't exist. I have invented him. Not just in the sense that all memory is fictive – there is no original memory, we're always remembering that we're remembering – but because I needed a story to give shape to my own sense of loss. Perhaps I have invested so much in loss that I'm afraid of losing it. Is that possible? Can one really fear the loss of loss?

It's said that a myth is a story about the way things never were, but always are. Stories are all we have – all truth is told. Truth is not an event, it's a process. This is life, the struggle for the truth of yourself, and it won't come right, but something of it may become available to you in small portions. As for my father, the truth is: he loved us to bits, with the bits of himself that could.

Tomorrow I'm going to gather up all the documents and letters, the photographs and stamp albums with their identity parades of the dead, and take them in a suitcase to Peter's house. I'm going to pull the ladder down and climb into the attic, and place my suitcase next to my father's suitcase. And then I'm going to make my way home.

LIST OF ILLUSTRATIONS

All images copyright © Frances Stonor Saunders, unless otherwise stated.

NOTES AND SOURCES

13   **'the record of what's left on the record'**: Hilary Mantel, Reith Lecture, 2017, Part One; https://www.bbc.co.uk/programmes/b08tcbrp.

15   **halfway down the stairs**: A. A. Milne's 'Halfway Down':

> Halfway down the stairs
> is a stair
> where i sit.
> there isn't any
> other stair
> quite like
> it.

16   **Excursions further afield**: Most of this wonderful descriptive detail of a childhood in Romania in the 1930s is drawn directly from Roy Redgrave's memoir, *Balkan Blue* (London, 2000). I am deeply indebted to Roy's sons, Alexander and Robin, for permission to use this material so freely.

27 'an elegant, elegantly scuffed piece of luggage': Nabokov described the pigskin valise in an interview published by American *Vogue*, 5 April 1972.

28 'lucrative patterns of frustration': W. H. Auden, 'In Memory of Sigmund Freud', *Collected Shorter Poems: 1927–1957* (London, 1966).

29 But that's another story: much of this is related in my mother's memoir, whose opening line – '"Heil Hitler!" shouted Mummy as she pushed Daddy down the stairs' – brilliantly sets the tone. Julia Camoys Stonor, *Sherman's Wife: A Wartime Childhood amongst the English Catholic Aristocracy* (Desert Hearts, 2006).

30 'Did one *have* to have a parent?': Sybille Bedford, *Jigsaw: An Unsentimental Education* (London, 1999), Introduction p. x.

35 'The summons to complete the task of our forefathers': Tony Judt, 'From the House of the Dead: On Modern European Memory', *New York Review of Books*, 6 October 2005.

36 a clue in his naturalisation file: Joe's naturalisation file is in the National Archives, London: 'Słomnicki, Joseph, from Poland', HO144/1688/406734.

37 'Romania needs a face': quoted in Leslie Gardiner, *Curtain Calls: Travels in Albania, Romania and Bulgaria* (London, 1976), p. 120.

38 'round and perfect': quoted in Gilles Palsky, 'Emmanuel de Martonne and the Ethnographical Cartography of Central Europe (1917–1920)', *Imago Mundi*, Vol. 54, 2002, p. 113. In my grandparents' lifetime, Romania's territorial borders expanded and contracted repeatedly. Think of it as a mollusc, or systole and diastole. These alterations can best be seen in the animated map of

Romania on Wikipedia: https://protect-eu.mimecast.com/s/JCdNCYW7mcjrAgPC0cqd2?domain=en.wikipedia.org https://en.wikipedia.org/wiki/Territorial_evolution_of_Romania#/media/File:RomaniaBorderHistoryAnimation_1859-2010.gif

38   'There (in that heavy tapestried room)': Harold Nicolson, *Peacemaking, 1919* (London, 1933), p. 329.

39   'It would take a huge monograph': quoted in Palsky, 'Emmanuel de Martonne', p. 113.

40   the celebrations marking this success: Romania's celebrations at the conclusion of the war did not all end well. In 1919 King Ferdinand made a triumphant entry on horseback into a jubilant Bucharest, passing through an Arc de Triomphe erected to the glory of Romania. More arch than triumph, it collapsed shortly afterwards.

43   'I grew up ... in the belief that our glory': quoted in Hannah Pakula, *Queen of Roumania: The Life of Princess Marie, grand-daughter of Queen Victoria* (London, 1989), p. 39.

43   'sacrificing elegance for patriotism': quoted in 'A Trip to Constantinople – Across Roumania', unsigned article in *The Times*, 3 November 1883.

43   'like Emmenthaler cheese': quoted in Gardiner, *Curtain Calls*, p. 122.

45   'a Hollywood ensemble': quoted in A. L. Easterman, *King Carol, Hitler, and Lupescu* (London, 1942), p. 89.

45   laundered out of the country: Allegations of Carol's corruption were hotly contested after his abdication by his small clique of supporters, who argued, somewhat inconsequentially, that Carol cannot have been that rich, as he had appealed to friends for funds to support his life in exile. But isn't that what all royals do?

62   'the greatest defensive system ever devised': *Illustrated London News*, 6 April 1940, p. 452.

62   'the essential points of the French system': *Illustrated London News*, 29 October 1938, p. 794.

63   'has set a fashion followed all over Europe': ibid.

63   'Not one foot of Romanian territory shall pass': 'Rumania's Two Great Moats', *The Observer*, 21 January 1940.

63   'a living wall against aggression': ibid.

64   '"rivers of fire"': *Illustrated London News*, 2 March 1940, p. 283.

65   'They creep from their huts': Gregor von Rezzori, *The Death of My Brother Abel* (London, 1985), pp. 82–3.

65   'waiters bring ball-shaped chocolate cakes': Olivia Manning, *The Balkan Trilogy* (London, 2004), p. 126.

66   'Swarms of Berlin League of German Maiden girls': Friedrich Reck-Malleczewen, *Diary of a Man in Despair* (London, 2000), p. 68.

66   'held tight to his belt buckle': von Rezzori, *The Death of My Brother Abel*, p. 620.

67   'As to how 115 million ethnic Germans': *The Times*, 29 April 1939, 'Text of Herr Hitler's Speech', in which Hitler is quoted as saying, 'Nearly 115,000,000 people have been robbed of their right of self-determination.'

68   'every nation normally puts its demons': Reck-Malleczewen, *Diary of a Man in Despair*, p. 117.

68   'I thought of the hideous suffering': quoted in Pakula, *Queen of Roumania*, p. 286.

73   'At Buchs, on the Swiss-Austrian border': Edward Stonor, 'The Passing of Austria: Impressions of a Visitor', Letters to the editor, *The Times*, 4 April 1938.

74   'I once went there with Minka': Gregor von Rezzori, 'Troth', in *Memoirs of an Anti-Semite* (London, 1983), p. 234.

76 **were you the Israel Armin Freudmann**: the search for Armin Freudmann and Robert Fischer was conducted on Yad Vashem's Central Database of Shoah Victims' Names, www.yadvashem.org.

78 **'who had survived a northern natural catastrophe'**: Bettina Arnold, 'The Past as Propaganda', *Archaeology*, Vol. 45, No. 4, July/August 1992, pp. 30–37.

78 **'Early Germanic period'**, etc.: ibid.

79 **'Why do we call the whole world's attention'**: quoted ibid.

79 **'The one and only thing that matters'**: quoted ibid.

80 **'My father made sure'**: Redgrave, *Balkan Blue*, p. 27.

81 **even if Ovid had thought so**: Ovid would have approved of King Carol's beating of the bounds. The poet took very seriously the sacred function of borders, whose protection was placed under the patronage of the god Terminus, without whom 'there would be endless quarrel about land'.

82 **'They were Polish refugees'**: Redgrave, *Balkan Blue*, p. 28.

83 **'No enemy will ever be able to trample'**: quoted in *The Times*, 7 January 1940.

85 **'It was like a big fair'**: Mihail Sebastian, *Journal 1935–1944*, trans. Patrick Camiller (London, 2001), p. 240.

86 **'Not a word of the disturbing events'**: Redgrave, *Balkan Blue*, p. 23.

87 **'Theirs was a strategic position'**: R. G. Waldeck, *Athene Palace: Hitler's 'New Order' Comes to Rumania* (Chicago, 2013), pp. 58–9.

93 **'she walked across the square'**: Manning, *The Balkan Trilogy*, pp. 262–3.

94 **'Every morning the passers-by'**: ibid., p. 267.

94 **'No one was much impressed'**: ibid.

94 **'Harriet said: "There's a new map in the window"'**: ibid., pp. 271–2.

95   'Every day the crowd': ibid., p. 287.

96   'When [Harriet and Clarence] drove up': ibid., pp. 296–7.

96   '*Nous vaincrons parce que*': quoted in Heinz Soffner, 'War on the Visual Front', *The American Scholar*, Vol. II, No. 4, Autumn 1942, p. 469.

98   'a sort of tinned Occident': Vesna Goldsworthy, *Inventing Ruritania: The Imperialism of the Imagination* (London, 2013), p. 103.

102   **three and a half million civilians – ethnic Germans**: As agreed with the Soviets, Bessarabia's ethnic German population was repatriated to the Reich. In this way about 90,000 people carrying fifty kilograms of personal belongings found themselves, according to Nazi propaganda, 'voluntarily' and joyfully evicted from their homes. They were relocated in camps and barracks festooned with portraits of Hitler and swastika banners, assessed according to a racial 'quality inspection' and then 'returned' to the homeland they had never seen.

102   **'people who [had] grown out of their soil'**: von Rezzori, *The Death of My Brother Abel*, pp. 82–4.

103   **'They were greeted in the main square'**: Ladislau Löb, quoted in https://www.tikvah.ro/en/holocaust/northern-transylvania. Shortly after the Hungarians arrived, Löb jumped up to touch a Hungarian flag, 'just for fun'. This was reported to the police, and his father was taken to court and heavily fined because his Jewish son had insulted the Hungarian nation. His father later bribed a police officer and they escaped to Budapest, from where they were eventually deported to Belsen. Löb survived, and was later Emeritus Professor of German at the University of Sussex and translator of, inter alia, Béla Zsolt.

104 'the first light was kindled': M. Lugoshianu, former Transylvanian Minister, quoted in *The Times*, 2 September 1940.

105 'all my possessions': Béla Zsolt, *Nine Suitcases*, trans. Ladislaus Löb (London: 2005), p. 9.

105 'My whole life's work fits into one suitcase': quoted in T. J. Demos, 'Duchamp's *Boite-en-valise*: Between Institutional Acculturation and Geopolitical Displacement', *Grey Room*, No. 8, Summer 2002, p. 7.

107 'the international, criminal Jewish clique': quoted in Easterman, *King Carol, Hitler, and Lupescu*, p. 157.

107 Carol's private diary: Prince Paul of Hohenzollern-Roumania, *King Carol II: A Life of my Grandfather* (London, 1988), p. 191. King Carol was off the throne but he was not off the stamps bearing his portrait, which continued to circulate after his son succeeded him for the second time – proof that the currency of one reality is not always easily replaced by another. The past survives, *overrules*, its pastness. It was the same for Carol's son: in Donald's albums, stamps of Michael, the new (adult) king, are placed alongside stamps of Michael, the former (boy) king.

110 'I had seen the Iron Gates': Kim Philby, *My Silent War* (New York, 1968), p. 12.

112 'They were the salt of the earth': Geoffrey Household, *Against the Wind: An Autobiography* (London, 1958), p. 103.

112 'highly irregular procedures': the following events are documented in the National Archives, London: HS9/1481/6, HS9/1471/6, HS7/186, WO373/102/272, FO 371/24989, FO 371/24991/392, FO 371/24990. The arrests attracted intensive (and outraged) coverage in the British press. My principal source has been *The Times*. I am also indebted to Dennis Deletant, *British*

Clandestine Operations in Romania During the Second World War (London, 2020).

119 **'On the wall at the head of the marriage bed'**: Günter Grass, *Peeling the Onion* (London, 2008), p. 234.

132 **'If you ever have to make the same trip'**: quoted in Redgrave, *Balkan Blue*, p. 37.

132 **'We all have our troubles'**: quoted ibid., p. 38.

133 **'Micheline, tell Robin he *must* leave'**: ibid., p. 41. Rica (Maria) Antonescu had been a long-term friend of Micheline. Her own and her husband's signatures appear several times in the Doftana guest book in the decade before the general unseated King Carol. Rica thought she could be First Lady to a military dictator who embraced Hitler and still remain friends with Micheline. After Micheline left Bucharest, she sent some expensive chocolates to her girls, prompting Micheline to write, 'I wish she had not done so.' Under Rica's husband's dictatorship, Romania, alone with fascist Croatia, claimed the dishonour of having organised its own Final Solution, on its own initiative and under its exclusive control.

An estimated 200,000–300,000 Romanian Jews died. Antonescu was later executed, though not for this crime, and Rica was imprisoned in 1950 by the communist regime on the charge of 'bringing disaster to the country' (again, nothing to do with the murder of Jews). She was held in solitary confinement for five years, allowed to step out of her cell only at night, when she would collect and smoke the cigarette butts discarded by the guards. It's possible that Micheline took pity on her old friend – Rica had, after all, saved her husband Robin's life, but I've no idea if she reached out to her after the war.

136 'garbage, dung, stench and slander': George Seferis, 'Days of April '43', *Collected Poems, 1924–1955* (Princeton, 1981).

136 'All the waste-lots of the city': ibid.

137 'cripples, deformities': quoted in Artemis Cooper, *Cairo in the War: 1939–1945* (London, 2013), p. 79.

137 And there was the Gezira Sporting Club: Some Westernised Arab families were given membership to the Gezira Club, usually the kind who hired English nannies and French governesses. Edward Said's Palestinian father had a family membership, but this didn't protect his young son from the club's Honourable Secretary, Mr Pilley, who wore a pith helmet and patrolled the grounds on his bicycle. One evening, as Said was walking out of the grounds to go home, Mr Pilley accosted him: '"What are you doing here, boy?", he challenged me in a cold, reedy voice. "Going home," I said, trying to be calm as he dismounted from his bicycle and walked toward me. "Don't you know you're not supposed to be here?", he asked reprovingly. I started to say something about being a member, but he cut me off pitilessly. "Don't answer back, boy. Just get out, and do it quickly. Arabs aren't allowed here, and you're an Arab!" If I hadn't thought of myself as an Arab before, I now directly grasped the significance of the designation as truly disabling.' Edward Said, *Out of Place: A Memoir* (London, 2000), p. 44.

141 'the fat playboy': Olivia Manning, quoted in Deirdre David, *Olivia Manning: A Woman at War* (Oxford, 2013), p. 124.

142 'I cannot tell you how I long for peace': Redgrave, *Balkan Blue*, p. 99.

143 'Letter today from my dear one': ibid., p. 54.

144 'slinging the luggage aboard': Manning, 'Cairo: Back from the Blue'.

148 'accompanied at the piano': Said, *Out of Place*, p. 38.

148 'mystifyingly English': ibid., p. 39.

148 'an elderly bearded gentleman': ibid., p. 39.

149 'this meant bright and beautiful England': ibid., p. 82.

155 'He scrawled on a pad': Anthony Burgess, *On Going to Bed* (New York, 1982), p. 22.

157 'we cannot live together with them': quoted in Alan Adelson and Robert Lapides (ed.), *Łódź Ghetto: Inside a Community under Siege* (New York, 1989), p. 173.

160 **Middle East Relief and Refugee Administration**: MERRA, founded in 1942 by the British, evolved into the United Nations Relief and Rehabilitation Agency, or UNRRA.

161 **the dazzlingly talented pianist Maria Donska**: Maria Donska, born in Łódź in 1912, emigrated to England in the mid-1930s to escape the rising anti-Semitism in her country. After the fall of Poland she suffered a nervous breakdown, brought on by fears for the fate of her family. By 1943 she had recovered sufficiently to perform at the National Gallery's morale-lifting lunchtime concerts. She died in Kent in 1996. None of her family survived the Holocaust.

166 'no tumbledown castles': Johann Wolfgang von Goethe, 'America, you are better off'. https://erickoch.wordpress.com/2011/08/18/america-you-are-better-of/

168 'Like Rumkowski, we too are so dazzled': Primo Levi, *Moments of Reprieve* (London, 2002), p. 172.

168 'not tired from the walk': ibid., p. 159.

169 'He had understood many things': quoted in Gabriel Motola, 'Primo Levi: His Life and Death', *European Judaism: A Journal for the New Europe*, Vol. 21, No. 2, 1998, p. 45.

169 **'I am alone'**: Primo Levi, *The Reawakening* (New York, 1995), pp. 207–8.

174 **two other primary sources**: Details of Joe's entanglement in the communist takeover of the oil industry are taken from several files in the National Archives, London: FO371/72443 ('An Account of the Case of Mr Slomnicki'), FO371/2442, FO371/95003. There is also a substantial record of the affair at the British Petroleum Archive, Warwick University: ArcRef 18850 (Steaua Romana British Ltd); ArcRef 113391 (Steaua Romana General); ArcRef 51741 (Steaua Romana, Turkey, Austria and Greece, Claim by Steaua British Part 1); ArcRef 69051 (Steaua Romana British Ltd Minutes of Board Meetings, General Correspondence).

177 **the summer villa of Prince Ştirbei in Braşov**: Prince Barbu Ştirbei had died of liver cancer in 1946. His wife and eldest daughter managed his estates, including his eponymous wine business, until the communists expropriated them, along with the entire Ştirbei fortune, in 1949. Another of Ştirbei's daughters, Elise, was godmother to Donald. In the 1970s he tracked her down to an address in Germany and wrote to ask if he could visit her. She was delighted to hear from him, but begged him not to come, writing that she was a poor old lady now and would rather he remember her as she had been in happier days. She died in 1994. In 2001 Prince Ştirbei's vineyards and cellars were restored to his heirs by the Romanian authorities.

177 **other purged employees**: Joe's colleagues were among the estimated 300,000 Romanians who perished in the communist Gulag between the late 1940s and mid-1960s. I am grateful to John Laughland, Vlad Eker's grandson, for sending me a copy of Vlad's short

unpublished memoir. Accounts of the bottomless hole of Romania's prison system in this period are few and far in English translation, which makes Gheorghe Tomaziu's *The Witness* (translated, edited and published by Jane Reid, London, 2015) all the more compelling.

200 **'every happy man'**: as quoted by George Saunders, *Daily Telegraph*, 18 October 2017.

201 **'all sorts of ballads and folk tales'**: C. S. Lewis, *A Grief Observed* (London, 2013), p. 48.

ACKNOWLEDGEMENTS

ORIGINS

I owe a great debt to Craig Raine and Carmen Callil for including a piece about my father's death in *New Writing 7* (British Council/Vintage, 1998), which they co-edited. More than twenty years on, I reread the piece and realised I had found the opening to this book. I thank Craig for many years of spirited encouragement and his jeweller's eye for detail. Carmen, too: she is an indispensable first reader, and how patiently she has listened to my every jeremiad about the sheer difficulty of writing (between us, we have elevated this grievance into an art form).

It was Carmen who introduced me to Mary-Kay Wilmers, editor of the *London Review of Books*, in whose pages a distilled version of this book first appeared in the summer of 2020. Mary-Kay was bold to commission those pieces from the most speculative of proposals, a decision that followed from an earlier, even bolder suggestion that I give one of the *LRB*'s Winter Lectures in 2016. The lecture explored the meaning and impact of borders in our lives, with specific reference to the refugee crisis. I didn't know it at the time, but the title, 'Where on Earth are you?', was really a question directed at my father. My thanks also to Jean McNicol and Paul Myerscough at the *LRB*.

BBC Radio 4 was another home for my growing obsession with borders, in the form of a three-part series, *Borders: An Odyssey*, broadcast in 2016. Another impulsive commission, given my vagueness as to what the series might contain. Thank you, Innes Bowen, Mohit Bakaya and Fiona Leach, my producer, who made me read Homer's *Odyssey* (the founding text of everything, I now understand) and crafted a beautiful extended radio essay. Fiona also read an early draft of this book and saved me from a catalogue of embarrassments. We have become fast friends, the greatest reward of any journey.

Further inspiration came from Michaela Crimmin, co-director of Culture+Conflict, who invited me to take part in a panel event at the Institute of Contemporary Arts in December 2016. The subject was 'Promised Land' (I had hoped to reach it), and I chose to give a short talk about the dilemmas confronting people who have to flee their home: principally, where to go and what to take. This was the seed for an exhibition at the 12 Star Gallery in Europe House, London, which opened in December 2018. *What Would You Take?* was commissioned by Jeremy O'Sullivan, then cultural attaché of the European Commission Representation in the UK. The exhibition was a collaboration with the Estonian photographer Kaupo Kikkas, whose talent for capturing both the resilience and the vulnerability of people who have experienced displacement left us all speechless. It was a great privilege to work with him.

What Would You Take? subsequently travelled across London as an installation in Studio Egret West. For this version we introduced a prototype travelling bag designed with migrants in mind – a multifunctional, all-in-one kit pack, inspired by the famous Swiss penknife, that answers to the very particular requirements of having to carry your life on your back. Many thanks to Christophe Egret, Freddie Jackson, Malene Igland, Theo Games Petrohilos, Carlos Quinones.

I'm hugely grateful to Bea Hemming, my editor at Cape, for her close and sympathetic attention to the manuscript, which was greatly improved as a result. I met Bea by chance in a restaurant, when she was having lunch with Peter Straus. It was Peter who waved me over and made the introduction that led to this book finding its publisher, for which I am very lucky. My thanks also to my agent, Felicity Rubinstein.

In one way and another, these were all encouragers, and I hope this book does not diminish their faith in me.

RESEARCH

For their kind assistance, my thanks to the staff of British Petroleum Archive, Warwick University; the National Archive, London; the Wiener Library, London; Yad Vashem; the International Tracing Service. Special thanks to Dennis Deletant for his work on British intelligence activities in Romania during and after the Second World War; John Laughland, for sending me a copy of a short memoir written by his grandfather, Vlad Eker, who was a friend and colleague of my grandfather; Marie-Lise Cantacuzino-Ruhemann for talking to me about her Romanian child-hood, and the experience of exile; Alexander and Robin Redgrave, Roy Redgrave's sons, for access to his papers and family photographs and free rein on his evocative memoir, *Balkan Blue*, published in 2003; and Suzi Curtis, who kindly stepped in at the last minute to help with the diacritics on Romanian words.

BISCUIT TIN

A metaphor for reserves to keep me going. The biscuit tin was empty, and then my dear friend Nick Hewer filled it with the gains from another writing project – his memoir – which he insisted he needed help with. He didn't, but I'm so glad he asked. From the Royal Literary Fund came the most generous of grants. This was way back in 2010, at a time when I was completely derailed. I am relieved finally to have the opportunity to give public and heartfelt thanks for an intervention that rescued me.

HOME FRONT

For friendship and support beyond the call of duty, I am deeply indebted to my cousin and lifelong friend, Annoushka Ayton, and her husband John, and to Ann Pasternak-Slater, Lisa Allardice, Patsy Hickman, Lucy Heller, Domitilla Ruffo, Claudia Ruffo, my cousins Serban and Cristina Tiganescu, Amir Amirani, Fiona and Philip Marques, Jules Rey-Roeber, Mary Renouf, Anna Horsbrugh-Porter, Milan Nozka, Ulrike Chesney, Juliette Seibold, Christina Pribićević-Zorić, Enzo at Borgo di Ceri, and fellow traveller Carla Power. Also Zoë Heller, who has looked after me in so many ways. A friend since we were at university together, it was Zoë who asked me, after meeting my father, where he was from. A question I did not attempt to answer until now.

My uncle, Peter Saunders, suffered with great dignity all my nagging – and often difficult – questions. He has been an enthusiastic collaborator, a delightful host and a significant donor to the biscuit tin. This book would not have appeared without his support.

My mother, Julia Stonor, aka the Research Department, was a vital source of information, all of which she dredged up from her never-ending box folders and her laser-sharp memory. My thanks to her, and to my brothers Alexander and Hugo.

Lastly, I wish to thank Sylvia Millier for the gift of an ending. She will know what I mean.